The book you are holding in your ha█████████████████
Carey Casey has written. Period. He █████████████████
message in his heart because of the legacy he carries. It's just
now as a grandfather that he is able to say it. One line on
page 11 says it all: "But what shines for me in the lives of my
parents, grandparents, and great-grandparents is a persistent
practice of dignity, of rising above difficult circumstances,
and of quietly striving for a better life for those coming
later." As a grandfather of eight, I needed to be reminded
of these truths and the countless others that permeate this
book. Grandpa, read Carey's book and allow it to wash over
you with grace, love, and encouragement. A *Championship
Grandfathering* movement is right around the corner! And
my brother Carey Casey is at the tip of the spear!

DR. GARY ROSBERG
Cofounder, America's Family Coaches; author, *6 Secrets to a Lasting Love*;
speaker, radio broadcaster, and marriage and family advocate

Being a grandfather of three is among the highest callings,
blessings, and responsibilities God has given me. Carey
Casey's *Championship Grandfathering* is a strong gift,
equipping me and all grandfathers in this vital role. Carey's
experiences as a grandfather—and as the great man of faith
he is—come alive in these pages. Having served beside
Carey on the board of the National Center for Fathering
and seen him be a grandfather, I am grateful to have this
daily reminder of his stories and instructions as I attempt
to be the best grandfather God would have me be.

LEE PARIS
CEO, Meadowbrook Capital; board chairman, National Center
for Fathering

Carey Casey continues to show us the way through stories and practical examples. This book helps us to be champions as grandfathers.

DR. WAYNE "COACH" GORDON
Founding pastor of Lawndale Community Church and Chairman of the Christian Community Development Association

Foreword by
TONY EVANS

CHAMPIONSHIP
GRANDFATHERING

— How to Build a Winning Legacy —

CAREY CASEY

WITH NEIL WILSON

Tyndale House Publishers, Inc.
Carol Stream, Illinois

FOCUS ON THE FAMILY® | FOCUS ON PARENTING™

Editor: Julie Buscho Holmquist
Cover design by Ron Kaufmann

For information about special discounts for bulk purchases, please contact Tyndale House Publishers at csresponse@tyndale.com or call 800-323-9400.

Library of Congress Cataloging-in-Publication Data can be found at www.loc.gov.

ISBN 978-1-58997-874-4

Printed in the United States of America

23	22	21	20	19	18	17
7	6	5	4	3	2	1

To my nine wonderful grandchildren: Salem, John-John, Cora, Aniston, Sarah, Adelyn, Vivienne, Johnathan, and Ralph. I am so thankful to God for allowing me to live out Psalm 128:6: "And may you live to see your children's children." Pi-Pa and Grandma Casey are truly blessed every time we hear your playful steps in our home.

CONTENTS

FOREWORD

DECEMBER 25, 2012. Our family was together on Christmas morning, just hanging out, having fun. Gifts were still wrapped and under the tree. Pillows and blankets were scattered around the living room, and grandkids ran around in their pajamas. Someone turned on some holiday music with a good beat, and I just did what came naturally. I danced!

My daughter turned on the video camera app on her smart phone, and then she kept encouraging me: "Go, Papi. Show us what you've got." For a minute, I got caught up in it. I'm no Gregory Hines, although I might surprise you. She uploaded the video on YouTube, so now it's there for the whole world to see. She labeled the video "The Dancing Grandfather."

As I watched that video, at first I was embarrassed. I certainly don't come off as a dignified biblical scholar and respected pastor. But then, maybe there's no better portrayal of who I am. The moment was so *real*. I was in my element, celebrating the birth of Christ with the people I love the most, and when the music came on, it only made sense that the joy inside me would come out.

I get that way quite often when my grandkids are around. Few things put that spring in my step like having my grandkids nearby; they energize me in the best way. Their parents know they can bring the grandkids over anytime, and Lois and I will welcome them with open arms. Those youngsters always seem to bring out the best in me.

To a large degree, that's what this book is all about—that joy of relating to and investing in our children's children. I can't explain it, but it sure is rewarding and fun, and I hope reading these pages will help you celebrate that.

Of course, as my friend Carey rightly points out repeatedly in this book, the goals of a grandfather should be much bigger than just being a happy, dancing playmate for his grandkids. Like every other area of life, we should have a *Kingdom* focus with our grandchildren.

Training and shaping children to follow Christ is difficult in today's world, and when we reinforce the good things our children are teaching our grandchildren, that can be powerful in their lives. We often have different ways of explaining the simple truth of God's Word. We have stories about His faithfulness and mercy through the years. We have our own ways of living out Christ's calling to service and ministry. Through it all our grandchildren are watching and listening and taking mental notes, whether they realize it or not.

Our role modeling is so important. I hope my grandchildren think of their parents first if they ever ask, "What does it mean to live out the fruit of the Spirit?" But I also hope they see and remember how I was *patient* when I may have had a reason not to be, how I showed *kindness* to people in day-to-day life, how I *loved* people regardless of how they treated me, how I danced with *joy* on occasion, and so on.

I have often spoken and written about how parents need to instill those *Kingdom* virtues in their children—wisdom, integrity, faith, resiliency, purity, and service. That's up to parents first and foremost, but grandfathers can support and complement them in important ways.

I continue to be excited about the influence of Carey and the National Center for Fathering on fathers and families. You would do well to get your sons and sons-in-law plugged into their helpful insights and resources for dads and granddads.

I have eleven grandchildren, and their mere presence provides me with regular and very clear reminders that I am leaving a legacy. Like Carey, I am certainly not a perfect dad or granddad, but I have tried to be purposeful about how I invest myself in my offspring. They are your greatest legacy, and I hope you will find ways to make them one of your top priorities. There is no better way to spend your later years of life.

I am humbled at the ways God has blessed my children and grandchildren. They all are treasures in their own ways. And yes, they all bring me a lot of joy! Out of all the different reasons people might know me, "The Dancing Grandfather" is surely one of my favorites. And by the time this book is published, I will pick up an even better title: "The Dancing *Great*-Grandfather."

Tony Evans
PASTOR AND AUTHOR

A CALL TO ACTION

IF YOU'RE A DAD, there's a good chance you will be a grand-father someday.

Statistically, more than 90 percent of all Americans over age sixty-five whose children have reached adulthood have grandchildren. And most men who become grandfathers do so by age fifty. If you're like me, that sounds young. If you are already a grandpa, you might wonder what someone else has to say about the role.

Whether you're anticipating stepping into this new role or are already enjoying it, welcome to this great privilege and responsibility. When you're handed the ball called "Grandpa," don't drop it. If you have it, hang on to it.

Grandfathering, like fathering, is another important job

without a manual. Most of us didn't have any obvious training before we were presented with a child born from someone we clearly remember as a child.

Sure, there might have been people in our lives who provided a pattern for our own grandparenting efforts, but most likely we didn't pay attention to *how* we were trained. Or maybe our own grandparents were absent or disconnected from our lives, so they didn't offer much of an example.

Whatever our starting point, we probably didn't choose to become grandfathers the same way we chose to be dads. We were intimately involved in the process of fatherhood, but grandfatherhood is a possibility and title we are handed with little say-so on our part. Even so, the moment your excited son or daughter says, "Dad, you're going to be a grandpa!" or calls at midnight babbling, "Congratulations, Gramps!" you are changed in an instant, no matter how you've prepared for the moment.

I'm hoping you've made some great memories between your children's birth and his or her graduation into parenthood. In fact, I pray you've been a Championship Father. Now it's time to figure out what it takes to be a Championship *Grandfather*.

In 2009 I had the honor of authoring a book called *Championship Fathering*. That book was and continues to be a statement about the purpose of all we do at the National Center for Fathering, an organization I have been privileged to lead. I was delighted when Focus on the Family, the publisher of the original book, asked us to write this book about the next phase of life for fathers. Apparently, Focus on the Family realizes that the first Baby Boomers—the largest generation in US history—started turning 65 in 2011.[1] It seems likely that more and more of us are entering grandparenthood.

In preparation for this book, I reread *Championship Fathering*. If you haven't read it yet, let me encourage you do to so. I want to impress upon you that if your shortcomings and failures as a father are driving you to be a better grandfather, don't overlook the unfinished work of fathering. You may have added a new title to your portfolio, but you haven't been released from significant duties in the lives of your children. You'll still be Dad beyond your last breath. Much more on this later.

While revisiting *Championship Fathering*, I was surprised by how often I included asides to grandfathers or acknowledged that the principles shared in that book would apply to their grandchildren. We'll expand on those principles and map out some strategies in the pages to come. But for now, here at the beginning, let me call you to action as a grandfather.

As you read this book, you might discover that you're already doing many things right as a grandpa and have already responded to that call! I know that every grandfather I talk to is potentially a source of great wisdom for me. We need to share our discoveries with each other and definitely encourage each other along the way. Never hesitate to say to a grandfather who's doing something right, "Way to go, Grandpa!"

But I also believe that in the coming chapters you'll find a few ways to fine-tune your grandfathering "vehicle" so it runs better and safely carries your grandchildren to good places.

One of the joyful tasks I have in my family settings is

to surround our meals and gatherings in prayer. I want my grandchildren to say, "Grandpa prayed." So let me end this brief introduction with a prayer for you as you read this book and renew your commitment to be a Championship Grandfather:

Heavenly Father, let each man reading this book be encouraged; let each man know with clarity what's pleasing to You and what needs to be left behind. Lift up a fellow grandfather who's grieving lost years or missed opportunities, and show him what might still be done. Father, we all fall short of Your perfect example both as fathers and as grandfathers, but with Your help we can do better. Please convince us of that truth wherever we find ourselves today. Thank You for Your grace that brings that truth to us. In Jesus' name, amen.

CHAPTER ONE

THE DAY I BECAME "PI-PA"

THE YEAR WAS 2007, but it still feels like yesterday. I'd become a grandfather for the first time, and I couldn't wait to announce it to the world! Here's how I described my thoughts and feelings during those days in one of my radio ministry's "daily thoughts."

> Let me tell you, being CEO of the National Center for Fathering is nothing compared with my brand new title . . . Granddaddy! That's right. My son Marcellus and his bride recently had a baby girl, and I'm thrilled and humbled all at the same time.
>
> When we heard the news, one of my first thoughts was, *I have just become my father!* I'm

"Granddaddy Casey," just like my father was, and just like his father was before him.

The first member of the next generation of Caseys has already brought to me a renewed sense of responsibility. It's a new and exciting challenge. But it's an undertaking I am ready and eager to meet. My parents, grandparents, and great-grandparents prepared the way, and now it's my job to continue that legacy for this little girl.

I also think about this birth in the larger context of our culture. Here's what I mean: This baby girl met all four of her grandparents in the first forty-eight hours of her life! That's becoming less and less common today. What a blessing for that little one to have two parents and four grandparents who love her and who are there to help her grow into a godly woman.

Here at the National Center for Fathering, we believe that every child needs an involved dad, and those benefits extend down through the generations. It's a marvelous thing to be part of. I have done my best to pass a healthy legacy to my children, and now I get to watch and support them as they pass it on to their children.

Right after I found out about my granddaughter's birth, I was driving and listening to music, and I put in a CD by Nicole C. Mullen. One of her songs spoke to my heart in a fresh new way—it brought me to tears. Her song called "I Wish" captured my number-one dream for my new granddaughter.

The song paraphrases the words of the Great Commandment from Mark 12:30, and I just can't stop singing it: "Of all the things I could ever want for you, I wish this more than life: Love the Lord with all your heart, with all your soul, your mind, and strength."

Dad, that's the most important legacy you can ever hope to pass on to your children and their children.

Now that I've welcomed many grandchildren to the world, I read that account and chuckle. Mostly I was thinking about the changes that little baby girl brought into my life. When I said, "I've become my dad," I realized that with the birth of a new generation in my family I was one step closer to being history!

The weeks and months that followed that birth were filled with added lessons about the way one generation flows into the next. No one stops being a dad when he becomes a granddad. You simply add a completely new set of delights and duties. Both as a father and now as a grandfather, I've come to understand in a new way what Jesus meant when He said, "Everyone to whom much was given, of him much will be required" (Luke 12:48, ESV). The title of grandfather comes with responsibilities, and those of us who are ushered into that office had better figure out as soon as we can what the job requires of us.

My bride, Melanie, and I now have nine grandchildren, or as someone might call them, "a small riot about to happen."

Shunton and Christie (our eldest) have presented us with two grandkids, while our secondborn, Patrice, and her husband, John, have gifted us with three more. But our son Marcellus started the avalanche of little ones who have filled my bride's life and mine with a new level of joy, laughter, busyness, and exhaustion! He and Stephanie have added four members to our clan.

This means that we now have two nine-year-olds, three seven-year-olds, two five-year-olds, and two three-year-olds. For the moment, when everyone is present we have an adult for every grandchild in the family, counting our youngest child, Chance, as one of the grown-ups. But when it's just Melanie and me with the nine grandkids, it's easy to see how we might feel outnumbered! I'm so glad my bride is a teacher and not at all intimidated by a room full of kids.

Pi-Pa?

After talking with other grandfathers, I've discovered that the title given to me by my granddaughter Salem—Pi-Pa (pronounced PEE-PAW)—is not unique. I thought my creative grandchild had invented a never-before-used term to describe who I was.

Kids *can* be creative, but in this case, the name probably has to do with the way little human beings learn how to speak and what sounds come easiest to them. One woman I know was called "Gonga" by her granddaughter. It's not a term that sounds special or endearing on its own, but the source made it precious to her. Whether it's Opa, Mmmpa, Grapa, Gonga, or Pi-Pa, one thing is true—our grandchildren can call us pretty much anything they want as long as they call us!

I know parents have the right to expect their kids to talk

to them first, but I also know that having that little child recognize you as someone special and run into your arms is an unforgettable experience. Those trusting smiles, giggles, and hearty laughter bring sunshine into any gloomy day.

And let me tell you, when you have nine grandchildren at your house when you come home from work, and they stampede to hug and greet you, that's an experience beyond words. They already know that after the first round of hugs and kisses (including one for my bride), Pi-Pa will change out of his go-to-work clothes and put on his hang-out-with-the-grandkids-at-home clothes. They may watch *Mister Rogers' Neighborhood* on TV occasionally, but every time they're at our house they are learning about being part of Mr. Casey's neighborhood.

Grandma is the activities coordinator; Pi-Pa is the benevolent supervisor. He's the one in whose lap you can crawl for a break, or who can be convinced to be the foundation for a game of "Pile on Pi-Pa."

Sometimes the spotlight is on me. My bride will turn to me at the dinner table and say, "Let's have Pi-Pa say thanks over this meal." At those times, I'm happy to express my gratitude to God for the blessings *on* the table and *around* the table.

But mostly, I'm more like a living rock in the middle of the rushing river than someone keeping up with all that's going on. I'm watchful but content. One of my friends calls his times surrounded by his grandchildren "happy chaos," and I know what he means. But I'm also seeing that as my grandchildren grow older, the blur of activity is also broken up by little conversations, curious questions, and times of quiet in which one of the grandkids shares a moment on the recliner with the "rock." And that "rock" is happy for their company as he watches the next generation grow up.

Grand Changes

Don't get the idea from what I just described that I'm not actively involved in what's happening in my house. The grandkids aren't about to let Pi-Pa sit still for long. I'm a doting granddad, fortunate to still have a significant amount of energy. And I must say, having the flow of grandchildren around has given me a new awareness of the gift of life.

Take what happened just a few weeks after our first grandchild was born. My son and his wife were visiting us with their baby girl. One morning Melanie, Chance, and I were hurrying to get ready for a busy day. Concerned about being late, I was getting on everyone's case: "Why aren't you ready? We have to leave! I can't be late!" Then, when I thought we were all ready to walk out the door, I asked, "Where's Melanie?"

"Um . . . she's holding the baby," someone said.

"Holding the baby?" I responded excitedly. "You mean . . . she's awake?"

Suddenly my priorities changed. Surely we could spare a few minutes. And in a flash, I was right there at Melanie's side, making baby talk to my granddaughter. She opened her eyes, looked at me, and gave me a big smile.

Maybe it was gas, but I'm going with another explanation: There's a special bond—a magical connection—between a grandfather and his grandchild. You can hardly wait for the moment when the smile becomes a smile of recognition. When your grandchild knows you, something amazing has taken place. Another generation is starting to discover who they are and where they came from.

From a grandfather's view, there is great fascination in connecting with your own descendant. It's motivating and energizing! Having grandchildren brings out a side of us we never knew existed. My grandchildren's pictures are all over my smart phone, and I brag on them every chance I get. I can already tell that my grandchildren are going to accomplish great things for this world and for God's Kingdom. Another generation means all kinds of possibilities!

If you're a grandfather, you know exactly what I mean. It's a special, rewarding time. And what's even better is that our job isn't just about making baby talk. We have a unique role to play.

Without stepping on our children's toes as they learn to be parents, we also have a new round of responsibilities. We impart values. We see the big picture. We offer an older and wiser perspective on the world. And we should intentionally exercise this strength as we try to be Championship Grandfathers. And as I experienced, we're more likely to put other things on hold so we can soak up all the joy of investing in our loved ones.

Start with a Tree

Your grandchildren or soon-to-come grandchildren may motivate you to be the best grandpa you can be, but they can't give you much guidance on how to do the job. In other words, grandkids don't come with instructions. The fact that you're reading these words means you're interested in a little direction, so let's get started.

First, I'd like to remind you that this isn't your first rodeo! Expect to take some of your cues from your failures and successes in fathering. But it's important to know that this additional position with your children's children doesn't let you off the fathering hook, and it's not simply a do-over with a new generation. If you don't pay attention and practice some soul-searching about the fathering job you've already done, you are most likely to repeat mistakes—something neither you nor I want to do.

Next, to begin this soul-searching, you need to consider the influence of family members who came before you. So instead of thinking about *yourself as a* grandfather, start thinking about *your own* grandfathers. What do you know about them? It's likely your grandfathers have already died. If this is not the case, you have a brief opportunity to mine gold. If your own father is alive, he can be a source of valuable information about your heritage. Conversations between generations of men in a family often don't occur naturally; they must be intentional.

One area of fruitful interaction is talking about previous generations. Asking your father (perhaps reeling from the reality that he is now a great-grandfather) about his memories of his dad and granddad may open up treasures of family stories you never knew. Even if his relationship with his father wasn't great, you can still learn about family dynamics. That knowledge can often help you understand things about yourself that may have been a mystery until now.

In the chapters to come, we'll talk about what we can learn from the past that will help us influence the next generations in a positive, intentional way. Understanding your heritage will influence the legacy you leave behind.

Finally, one way to start learning about that legacy is by creating a family tree. As a grandfather in your family tree, your life's branches have already sprouted leaves, better known as grandchildren.

A Champion Grandfather is aware of and appreciates his own heritage. The fact that you are alive means there's an unbroken chain of fathers reaching back from your life to the very beginning. Every link in that chain contributed in some way to who you are. Does that mystery intrigue you?

Even if you're only able to trace back four or five generations, you may discover some astounding facts about your heritage. The basics of creating a family tree include recording names, dates, relationships, and places. These four categories will add up to many facts, even in a small family.

You may be among the many guys who lose track of important dates, so creating this family tree might mean you'll have to make an effort. If you have trouble remembering your anniversary or your grandkids' birthdays, it's time to "man up" and either fill in an electronic calendar on your smart phone or buy a journal and name it "Dates I Don't Want to Forget."

Your bride will probably be stunned if you sit down beside her with your phone/tablet/journal and say, "Honey, I need to make a list for myself of important dates." You may discover she has a few generations of birthdays and anniversaries written down somewhere for you to copy.

Once you have names and dates of a couple of generations

before you, start working on a short profile of each person: place of birth, where they are buried, what kind of work they did, significant events in their lives, and any quotes, sayings, or traits that are attributed to them in the family. If you remember specific experiences you had with these people, make a note of them. Better yet, start an audio collection entitled "Things I Remember about My Family" that you can pass on to your kids and grandkids.

Let me add at this point that you may be a fortunate man. As you have conversations with your bride and various extended family members about your tree, ask if anyone in the clan has been compiling genealogical facts about the family. Someone may have done the work for you! If you discover charts that trace the branches of your family and your bride's family, you have a head start. Be sure to thank any living family members who have already done this work.

But realize these collections of names, dates, and relationships are just the framework that needs to be filled in with as many stories as you can find. Along the way, you may be amazed at other discoveries you make.

I have a friend who was born in 1950, the first grandson on his father's side of the family. When he was a teenager, his oldest uncle pulled him aside during a brief visit and gave him a military saber that was used by an ancestor during the American Revolutionary War. The rusty sword was still encased in a leather scabbard that was falling apart.

The oldest son in each generation of the family had been the keeper of that family heirloom. Unfortunately, that uncle died shortly after he passed on the sword, and the young man never learned of any specific stories or history connected with that object, a mystery he is still trying to unravel.

One tantalizing tidbit of family lore is that the saber was wielded by an officer who arrived in America as a mercenary hired by the British to fight the rebellious colonists. The officer deserted to the enemy and earned his citizenship by fighting in the Continental Army. Apparently, he abandoned his original name and adopted a new American name, which the family still bears.

The teenager who received that saber is now a grandfather himself, still trying to verify that story but enjoying the idea of being related to a Revolutionary War hero.

Like many Americans of African descent, I know my family tree eventually branches back across the ocean to Africa. Visiting that continent as an adult with my son, Chance, was a reminder that the story of my family has come a long—and sometimes very difficult—way. I have come to realize that generations have subtle but profound effects on those coming after.

Because of the circumstances of my ancestors' arrival in this country, much of my family history before emancipation is unknown. I know more about my family's history during the time following official slavery and in the continuing decades of latent racism in our country. There are plenty of stories among my relatives of places we couldn't go, hotels we couldn't stay in overnight, and dehumanizing treatment received.

But what shines for me in the lives of my parents, grandparents, and great-grandparents is a persistent practice of dignity, of rising above difficult circumstances, and of quietly striving for a better life for those coming later.

I'm a product of several generations of people who understood that making good use of an actual opportunity was much better than complaining about opportunities that were not there. It's gratifying for me to watch and listen to my grown children express their pride in what their grandparents and great-grandparents were able to achieve with limited choices. They are humbled to realize how much of their life stories were shaped by people in out-of-the-way places back in Virginia, people who worked hard and built a legacy for the family.

Part of that legacy is a phrase I can still hear my dad say over and over (I always say it with his intonation, a little deeper than my natural voice): "Son, you've got to remember the importance of perseverance."

The older I've become, the more I've seen that he was passing on to me what had been passed on to him. His father and grandfather had persevered. Likewise, my dad stayed on track in the little and big things, no matter what kind of obstacles or environment he faced.

His little one-word or one-sentence sermons influenced my life because that's the way he lived. I didn't see Pop telling me one thing and doing another. He highlighted his words with actions.

The stories I've been able to share with Marcellus about his grandfathers have aroused his curiosity. I have some of my father's journals, which my sister put into my care after Pop died. When they are missing from my study, I know Marcellus has borrowed them for some research. I can hardly tell you what it means to watch my son take an interest in his past.

Those journal pages seem at first to be covered with only "chicken scratches." But when I take a closer look at those notations, words start leaping off the page. I hear his voice— deep, mellow, and always thoughtful.

He considered words before he said them. He wasn't in a hurry. At times, it seemed as if he tasted the words before he said them. And he didn't have to talk a lot to say something meaningful.

When I started reading his journals, I realized that many things he had told me were not off-the-cuff thoughts. He had made notes to himself and chosen specific words he wanted to use.

So it doesn't surprise me that perseverance comes up often in his writings. He didn't stumble into perseverance. As an African American man, he had a deep appreciation for the perseverance of his forefathers, individuals who led to his life, his opportunities, and a way of conduct that could preserve generations to come. And when I see my son reading his grandfather's journals, I realize he's not only connecting with his heritage; he's also seeing in many ways why his father is the way he is.

Taking time to explore your own heritage will definitely give you a perspective on the generation or two immediately before you. It's not always an easy thing. We discover that certain patterns in our parents are actually good or bad echoes of previous generations. Later in the book, we'll talk about how we can make changes for the sake of future generations.

Sometimes digging into the past comes with humorous moments. My friend Neil had the joy of homeschooling his youngest child during her high school years. They decided that one of her ongoing projects would be family exploration. She was thrilled to discover she had a Canadian great-grandmother who had emigrated from Scotland when she was quite young.

These discoveries were made during the time that the movie *Braveheart* was released. One of the standing jokes between Neil and his daughter was watching the battle scenes and guessing which of their Scottish relatives might have been represented on the screen.

Tracing your family tree may include some dead ends or hard-to-find trails. What if you or a previous ancestor were adopted? The records might be difficult to access or completely lost. You have the choice to continue genealogical detective work or to actively "reverse adopt" the family who opened their doors to you. Accept their heritage as your own and be grateful that their family values included making room for those who had lost their family connection. They gave you a priceless gift, and that's a legacy in itself.

Action Steps

1. Create a personal family tree including at least your children; yourself and your wife; and the parents, grandparents, and possibly the great-grandparents on both sides. List names and birth, wedding, and any death dates for each.

2. Decide how you will develop a short profile for each of the names on your family tree. Give yourself a month to fill in the spaces.

3. Start with your own profile. What do you want your children to remember about you? What do you want your grandchildren to experience with you? I hope by the time you finish reading this book, your list of ideas in these areas will have grown.

CHAPTER TWO

WHAT IS CHAMPIONSHIP GRANDFATHERING?

BEFORE WE CAN TALK about the basics of Championship Grandfathering, we have to know and understand Championship Fathering. The two are definitely connected, just as the PGA Seniors Tour is a branch of the regular PGA Tour. You have to play pretty good golf to make it on the PGA tour; you have to play great golf for a long time to make it on the Seniors Tour. In my earlier book, here's how I defined Championship Fathering:

Dads involved in Championship Fathering know the fundamentals: loving, coaching, modeling. They apply those fundamentals to their kids and keep practicing them throughout the seasons of life. These dads also know they're part of a team and make encouraging connections with other team members.

Taking this definition into account, I describe Championship Grandfathering like this:

Grandfathers involved in Championship Grandfathering are well on their way to mastering the fundamentals: loving, coaching, modeling. They continue to hone those fundamentals with their grown kids and with the children of their children. They keep practicing the fundamentals throughout the seasons of life, building a legacy for future generations. These granddads also know they're part of a team and make encouraging connections with other senior team members.

I know the word *championship* can easily tie into our competitive natures, but Championship Grandfathering isn't a contest or competition. In fact, since there's probably at least one other grandfather in your grandchildren's lives, one of your tasks as an effective grandfather is to make the other one(s) look good. You want to teach those grandkids what it means to share? Show them by the way you graciously share them with other grandparents.

So what's the challenge of Championship Grandfathering? It's the challenge of being a much better grandfather than you would be if you just went with the flow and avoided thinking too much about your responsibilities. The very fact that you picked up this book and are trying to school yourself in this role says you're on the way to a championship season in life.

Does that mean that our goal is to get everything right all the time? That's not going to happen. What we want is to get some things right most of the time and most things right at least some of the time.

Grandfathering is definitely not precision work. It's not

a one-and-done proposition that gives you a single opportunity to do things right, and if you fail, it's over. It's a labor of love that includes plenty of mistakes and even more not-getting-it-as-right-as-we-wanted times.

Despite the fumbles, you'll be amazed at what kids gain just from your presence. You might not think you're contributing anything, but the way grandkids value that time is humbling! Grandpa, let me tell you that your grandkids will make you glad you tried to be grandfatherly even when you fail. They will help you experience joy you could never know if you were so afraid of failing at grandfathering that you never even tried!

Fundamentals

The definitions of Championship Fathering and Championship Grandfathering feature the term *fundamentals*. We'll explore each of these basics in detail later on. For now, I want to consider the *concept* of fundamentals. When you break down a sport or a job to its essential parts or skills required, the list is not usually long.

Take basketball, for example. The basics are dribbling, passing, and shooting. There's a lot more to the game, but if you can't dribble, pass, or shoot, it doesn't matter that you understand the "pick and roll" technique.

If you're a pilot, you have a checklist with certain items you need to be sure about before you take off. You're asking for trouble if you start skipping items on that list. You don't want to be the one saying, "Because I didn't check the flaps, I never realized one of the wings was missing." You know what I mean? That's a problem.

But I'm reminded of something I've noticed about consistently successful football programs. Right now one of the outstanding teams in the National Football League is the Green Bay Packers, coached by Mike McCarthy and quarterbacked by Aaron Rodgers.

In press conferences, the members of that team consistently state that they can always improve. To do that, they say, they must always return to the fundamentals. When they lose a game, the coach will invariably say, "We're going to look at the fundamentals again this week. We've let a couple of important skills slide."

Most of what you're going to read here is about fundamentals. I know your situation is unique, and it will take some attention to apply these ideas. But please realize that there are some basics to the task of being a grandfather that you can do, and you can do better.

As you grasp the fundamentals of loving, coaching, and modeling, it's crucial to keep asking yourself, "How can I step up my game in these areas? Who can help me see where I'm missing opportunities? How can I encourage other grandfathers so that I have a team around me who can encourage me, too?"

Old Dogs

At the National Center for Fathering, we notice that many older guys tune us out. As their kids grow older and more independent, they feel as if their fathering role is slowing down and they've probably learned just about all they can. You can't teach an old dad new tricks, right? Or they've just become grandfathers and they think it's coasting downhill from now on. I understand these feelings! It's easy to think that way.

On top of that, even young granddads can make the mistake of accepting these subtle messages of our culture: "Old dogs" can't learn "new tricks," it's too late to change, and you're too slow to "get it." The worship of youth in America has dangerously depleted the wisdom that comes with experience.

The fact that your grandkids may have to help you program your smart phone doesn't mean you can't give them help with life. It's okay to chuckle and admit you're "not as smart as a fifth grader," as long as you don't forget you still need to be wiser and deeper than that child.

When your son or daughter puts that baby in your arms, you realize how much she needs you. You might think that child doesn't require your services once she learns to walk and start school, but her need for you has only changed. Your grandchildren still need you, even if they forget sometimes.

Grandpa, be the one who doesn't forget. Be someone who gives your grandkids what they need even when they don't realize they need it or say they don't want it. Be the one who says, "I love you" in their ear when no one else can hear and they don't seem to listen.

I realize you might never have heard that phrase when you were growing up. Your parents and grandparents may not have known the value of saying, "I love you." But that doesn't make it unimportant, and the feeling of loss or lack you have right now is the best argument for that fact.

The past explains but doesn't excuse you from keeping

that tradition going. Be the old dog who starts some new tricks in your family. Be the "gray" that has something to say, even if it's "I love you" at unexpected moments that catch others off guard.

The other day, this "old dog" was inspired by Psalm 92:12-15:

> The righteous will flourish like a palm tree,
>   they will grow like a cedar of Lebanon;
> planted in the house of the LORD,
>   they will flourish in the courts of our God.
> They will still bear fruit in old age,
>   they will stay fresh and green,
> proclaiming, "The LORD is upright;
>   he is my Rock, and there is no wickedness in him."

Can you picture what this psalm is saying about you and me as grandfathers? Part of the idea of aging "like a cedar of Lebanon" is that at some point, you're going to be respectfully cut down, sawn into timbers, and become part of a structure that honors God. Will you age like that cedar? When your children and grandchildren look at and try to use the products of your life, will they find useful stuff?

Palm trees bear fruit; cedars bear boards. Both contributions are important. The difference reminds me of the well-known story of the chicken and the pig who were talking in the barnyard about what they could do to thank the farmer for the good life they were enjoying.

Finally the chicken said, "I know. Let's fix him a big breakfast with scrambled eggs and bacon!"

The pig answered, "Nice idea, but let's keep thinking."

"What's wrong with scrambled eggs and bacon?" the chicken replied. "It's a great breakfast, and both of us can make a contribution."

The pig said, "You're missing one thing. Eggs are your contribution, all right. But for me to contribute bacon takes a total commitment!"

Think of it this way: Like the palm trees, you're delivering fruit into your kids' and grandkids' lives; like the cedar tree, you are also giving yourself away to them. You're building into your loved ones a structure as real as boards and timbers that they will use when you're gone. They need your contributions *and* your total commitment. That's what Championship Grandfathering is all about.

Now believe me, I know how things change as you get older. In your career, you once were the young pup full of questions; now you're the old dog with all the answers. When the kids were young, you were too busy to play. Now that they're busy, you wish they'd come around a little more and bring the grandkids with them! The cycles of life catch up to you.

But whatever child/parent/grandparent phase of living you find yourself in now, it's worth asking this question: "Do the current pace and priorities in my life reflect what I say is important?" If your answer is "I'll start doing the important stuff tomorrow, or later, or when I retire," you're setting yourself up for disappointment and regrets. Today is always a good day to do something important. Putting it off to tomorrow probably means it won't happen.

Perspective changes, Granddad. You're in a different

chapter of life. As I talk to people with more life experience, one common theme I hear is that they are going deeper spiritually. They are seeing things now they didn't see years ago. Maybe because they know they will meet God sooner rather than later, the matters of eternity have become more important. I'm not preaching at you—yet. I'm just saying, "Grandpa, haven't you felt the shift in the way you look at things?"

I know that not all experienced dads are tuned out as fathers and going with the flow as grandfathers. Many of the most devoted men spreading the message of responsible fatherhood are older guys. They know dads matter! They're mentoring younger dads who might not really "get it" yet.

So if you're in that "older dad and the father of fathers and mothers" group with me, let me encourage you today. You're still needed! You're still vital! As the psalm says, you can still "bear fruit." That's true regarding your children and grandkids. You'll always be "Dad" and "Granddad." You can make powerful, positive investments in their lives.

This is also a great time to reach out beyond your family. Mentor someone. Meet with a younger dad for coffee every week. Get involved in a ministry at church. Teach a Sunday school class or lead a small group of middle school boys. You probably can't do all these things well, but if you have no idea what you can do, start experimenting. If you haven't discovered a "thing" that you do, it's time to get serious about finding it!

I know one grandfather who shows up for Sunday school every week, but he doesn't teach. He lets the person in charge of children's ministry assign him to a classroom where he sits and encourages the teacher by his presence. He answers kids' questions. He's mostly just there making a difference, often without saying anything.

Keep your eyes out for a neighborhood kid who needs a father figure or a fill-in grandpa. Get to know that child. I promise, it's one of the most rewarding activities you'll ever do. Remember: You have a storehouse of father power—one of the most valuable commodities on the planet.

Not a Pretty Picture

Look at the statistics: Back in 1960, about 9 percent of children in America lived with just one parent. In 1996, that number was up to 28 percent. Today, it's up to 34 percent—about 27 million children. So the number of father-absent children nearly quadrupled in less than sixty years!

If we don't do something, what will those numbers be like when our grandchildren are adults? Fifty percent fatherless kids? Sixty? Seventy? All the problems that come with fatherlessness would be magnified. I'm not sure we can even imagine the impact on the culture in terms of values, economics, crime, and family structure. How can we prepare our children and grandchildren for that?

Now you might be saying, "That's alarming, Carey. But I'm involved in my children's lives. I'm raising them to be responsible and God-fearing people. I see my grandkids regularly. I go to all their sports activities. They'll be okay."

I applaud you for that, but please don't underestimate the influence the culture can have on your children and grandchildren. Directly or indirectly, they will be influenced by peers, teachers, neighbors, lawmakers, musicians, and others in the media. These influencers will most certainly reflect the dominant culture of the day. And with the spread of social media, the influence on kids and grandkids is relentless. Young people are Snapchatting and texting 24/7 (many of them have moved beyond Facebook).

My grandkids don't have phones yet, but it will happen. If yours are already connected, how often do you send them a simple text to remind them you love them? The world will work hard to distract them from the truth and from what's right; decide that you will be a good distraction in their lives.

Of course, they're going to get hurt along the way. But we can keep reminding them where to find love and healing. As grandfathers, we need to step up our game and pass on our faith in persistent and deep ways to our grandchildren, seeking to counter the destructive aspects of our culture.

At the Center, we want to create a culture of Championship Fathering that will lead to widespread Championship Grandfathering, making a difference for generations to come. We want to jump-start a movement of men who will commit themselves to loving, coaching, and modeling for their children and grandchildren, encouraging other children, and then sharing the message with other dads.

The best expressions of fatherhood (and grandfatherhood) make a difference in the world, not just in one man's life or in one family. We live in a culture where there are plenty of discouraging trends concerning the welfare of children—and they don't bode well for the next generation.

If we're going to change the culture, we *all* need to take on a task that looks beyond ourselves.

This doesn't have to be difficult. One dad took his young son along with him to get the oil changed in his car. It was a chore Dad had to do, but he turned it into something more by having his son along. Without trying hard, he schooled his kid on the importance of taking good care of what we own so we can use it for a long time. He also had a chance to observe his boy in that setting to see if he had an interest in mechanical things. But more than all of that, they had the sheer delight of just hanging out together.

An older gentleman saw the two of them together. He was moved to hand the dad a few dollars, and told him to buy his son some ice cream. That grandpa gets it! You can be that grandpa who spots dads doing the right thing and steps in to quietly say, "You da man!" to that father. Coming from you as an older man, it will mean a lot.

Does this story inspire you to look beyond your own immediate circumstances? Maybe you feel called to work with dads more directly, and you have opportunities to speak or teach on fathering. Our training program at the National Center for Fathering (fathers.com) can help equip you for that. But you get the idea: Be positive about dads where you can.

As a grandfather, you can take the great step to give your children a break from their kids—for an evening, a few days, or a week—so they can get away, recharge, and strengthen their marriage.

If you and your bride raised your kids without much outside help, you know it was hard. In the past, grandparents, extended family, and the neighborhood worked together to raise kids. Daycare is not an equal substitute.

The Joy of Bonding

We'll talk more about this later, but I can't wait to share how time together creates a bond between grandparents and grandkids. I believe more and more that one reason to be a "great" dad is that being a "grand" dad is just around the corner.

Recently my daughter was visiting us with her husband and her baby boy, my grandson John-John. It was Sunday morning, and everyone was getting ready for church.

I was up early and was already dressed. And if I do say so, I had it going on—the tie was working, the colors were coordinated, and I had my "El Nerdo" pants pulled up high so that my well-shined shoes were in full sight.

John-John was dressed too, but he hadn't eaten yet, so his parents asked me to feed him breakfast.

"No problem," I said. "We'll have fun."

And we did. They put him in his high chair, strapped his full-coverage bib on, and turned me loose with the applesauce and that baby-sized spoon. John-John just sat there grinning at Granddad.

Before Melanie left the room to finish getting ready herself, she gave me one piece of advice: "Sweetheart, maybe you should take off your suit coat while you're feeding him."

I said, "Oh, no, babe, we're okay. He's got it down—look!" And I showed her how good I was at spooning the applesauce into his mouth.

He was just sitting there grinning at me with that

applesauce in his mouth, and then he went "pfffffttttt"—all over my suit and tie.

I should have listened to my bride, right? But John-John is a great little man. So I got real close to that boy and told him, "You're Carey Casey's grandson. Son, you can spit all over me."

That's my attitude. That's why I love it when all the grandkids come for Christmas and wreck the house, leaving Tupperware all over the kitchen. I admit it's a little easier to enjoy those times as a granddad because I don't have to deal with baby messes every day like dads do. At some point, the grandchildren go home and I start resting up for the next time. Dads don't have that luxury, but I still encourage them to enjoy every moment with their little ones.

Yes, it can get messy at times. But if you look for it—and expect it—you can even find joy in burping babies and changing diapers. Those are the moments that bond you for life, and they can happen at every stage of your grandchildren's lives.

Opportunity Cost

To master the art of Championship Grandfathering, we must realize there are costs and some hard choices involved. We have to remind ourselves to grab the moments of joy when they come and be intentional about them once we discover them. We need the reminders, because the best choice doesn't necessarily mean it's the easy choice. I know this from experience!

Not long ago I was working from home, catching up on phone calls and correspondence in my downstairs study. My task list was long, but I was really *plugged in*—getting important things done.

Then I heard the front door open upstairs, followed by that unmistakable pitter-patter of little feet running across the hardwood floor. Kids don't walk in a calm and relaxed way, right? They scamper and jump, especially when they've just arrived at Grandma's house.

I knew who it was—my daughter Christie and her son, my grandson, who was two at the time. I heard the pitter-patter and smiled, then went back to what was on my desk. Well, I *tried* to work. But I just couldn't focus. I felt myself drawn to that little boy like a magnet.

So I gave in. I thought to myself, *I have to be there right now. I don't want to miss these moments and opportunities. If you miss them, you can't get them back.* Besides, if I didn't go to him, he would eventually come looking for me. I wasn't going to wait.

I put my work aside for a few minutes and hurried upstairs for some fun with my little man. I held him, asked him some questions, and spent probably ten minutes interacting with him. As he's growing older, we're forming a unique relationship.

It was a great work break; there was no better way I could have spent that time. Even better, it reinforced the value of what I did when I went back downstairs. I could encourage fathers and talk about our work at the National Center for Fathering with a fresh passion and awareness of how important and rewarding parenting—and grandparenting—is.

You've probably heard about "opportunity cost." It's

often connected with money. The idea is that we have limited resources, so when we spend money on one thing, that removes the possibility of spending that money on something else. It's basic, but a good thing to keep in mind.

The principle also applies to our *time*. We have limited amounts of that, too, so when we choose to do one thing, we can't spend that time doing something else.

What does this mean to you as a granddad? I'm sure you're busy like me, and there's only so much time to get everything done at work and be with your family. But if you're not intentional about making time with your grandkids and putting time with them on your calendar, that inaction will result in *missed* opportunities.

Let me ask you this question: "What are your children or grandchildren going to remember about you?" Do they get your full attention on a regular basis, or are you working long hours and often just not there? Have they pretty much come to expect your absence?

Kids know you're busy. And that makes your time with them even more valuable—to you, and to them. Championship Grandfathering is learning to be the kind of man who looks for and takes advantage of opportunities with his grandkids. He even makes them happen. Let's explore ways we can move into the Championship Grandfathering zone.

Action Steps

1. In your family tree notebook, title a page "Five Intentions." What five main intentional actions do you carry out on behalf of your grandkids? List each and note two or three examples of each.

2. Reread the definition of Championship Grandfathering at the beginning of the chapter, taking
   note of the three fundamentals. Before we learn
   more about these basic components of effective
   grandfathering, note your understanding of them at
   this point. List the fundamentals below, and then
   rate your current status in mastering them from one
   to ten, one being "I only have a vague idea what that
   is" and ten being "Others are asking me to school
   them in that fundamental."

   a. 1————————5————————10

   b. 1————————5————————10

   c. 1————————5————————10

   Now plan one action for each fundamental that
   needs improvement. If you don't have a clue about
   what to do, ask another grandfather for help.

3. Make space for your grandchildren on your family
   tree, and then begin recording your observations
   about their unique characters. How is one grandkid
   different from the others in special ways? What gifts,
   talents, and perspectives has God built into each
   grandchild? This is spadework for later, when you
   will develop a blessing for each grandchild.

CHAPTER THREE

ENTER THEIR WORLD

Grandkids invade our space, and we need to invade theirs!

According to an AARP 2002 survey, most grandparents (56 percent) see at least one of their grandchildren every week, 12 percent see one of their grandchildren every two weeks, and 24 percent said they see a grandchild once a month to once every few months.

If you're a granddad who is already exceeding these stats, thank you! Take it from me—you are an incredibly valuable resource seldom used by our society.

We need to recognize and capitalize on the benefits that grandfathers can bring to children's lives. Grandpas are important because they symbolize family, they are living links between the present and the past, and they serve as connection points for the extended family.

If you need further incentive to step forward into your role as a grandfather, here's how Kirk Bloir from Ohio State University summarized a grandfather's place:

> Researchers have found that grandchildren who
> have a close relationship with a grandfather are
> likely to perform well in school, display positive
> emotional adjustment, have higher self-esteem, and
> a greater ability to develop and maintain friendships.
> Grandfathers who report having close relationships
> with grandchildren describe the significant joy they
> experience as a result of the unconditional love they
> feel for their grandchildren. Spending time with
> their grandchildren and displaying photographs
> of them provides reminders of their connection
> to future generations.[1]

To develop that close relationship, start entering your grandchildren's world at an early age. Don't just wait to be invited to help. Be proactive! Think of ways you can help. Volunteer to give Mom or Dad a reprieve, an hour or two of "me time" while you watch the kids. Your children may hesitate to ask you, but if you offer, they may jump at the chance for a breather.

Remember, you play a role in providing a healthy, loving environment for those grandkids long before they are consciously aware of you. As our nine grandchildren arrived, many times their two sets of grandparents were first responders on the scene. Get involved in their lives as soon as you can and stay there.

During their earliest years, you won't get much feedback

from the grandkids. That's okay. You can use your time to observe them, trying to see things they see and noticing how they respond. How they react even as babies often gives us clues to their characters and personalities.

If you have more than one grandchild, you will be constantly amazed at how different they are from one another. Make a note of these differences and keep them in mind as you relate to your grandkids. Your little granddaughter may love to sit with you and ask a thousand questions. Your grandson may want you to play trucks and make funny noises. Either one may love to color pictures for you or play house, store, or school. Or they may show an interest in things you wouldn't have immediately expected.

Ken Canfield, founder of the National Center for Fathering, describes the special grandfather-grandchild relationship this way:

> Who can explain what happens between a
> grandparent and grandchild? The grandfather sits
> down with his grandchild and tells stories no one has
> heard before—or stories everyone has heard many
> times, but they still enjoy the telling. Or, a child
> asks to see that trick where Grandpa somehow pulls
> his thumb apart, then puts it back together again.
> Others can try, but no one can do it quite like
> Grandpa.
>
> Earlier, Grandpa complained that his back
> was acting up after he dragged thirty pounds of
> garbage out to the curbside. But now, he can hoist
> his granddaughter up for a hug without a second

thought, without the slightest pain, almost effortlessly. Blake wants to go try to hook that big catfish in the creek, but he wants to wait until Grandpa can come, because only he knows where the "old monster" lives.

How do you explain it? You don't. You just enjoy it.[2]

Relating to Grandchildren

Because of the growing longevity in our society, more of the children being born today will be able to know their grandparents and great-grandparents. Whether or not you realize it, as a grandfather you bring a wealth of wonderful resources for your grandchildren to enjoy. Ken Canfield continues to inspire my own efforts at grandfathering with this question and practical list:

> What are the nuts and bolts of a relationship between a grandfather and his grandchild? At the risk of taking something magical, breaking it down and robbing it of its charm, here are some practical ideas: 1) make time; 2) do little things; 3) inspire and motivate; 4) transmit values.[3]

Let me unpack that list by adding lessons I've learned as I try to make this work in my family.

Make time

When you and I make time for the children of our children, we are using one of our secret weapons as grandfathers; it sets us apart from most of the other influences in our grandchildren's lives. They don't need to know we are being intentional, but we need to be intentional.

Many of us are transitioning into a time of life when we have more discretionary time or at least more flexible time commitments. This should help us make time to be in our grandkids' lives, but we will still need to schedule dates for individual or group activities with the kids.

One grandfather I know has a granddaughter who has shown interest in softball, excelling as a fifth grader in the skill of pitching, and mastering the sequence of body and arm moves required to deliver that windmill-looking throwing style.

For her birthday, her grandparents took her to a professional baseball game with all the trimmings. This involved a ninety-minute drive, dinner in the big city, seeing a few sites, an early arrival at the ballpark, the adventure of finding seats in a huge stadium, all the goings-on of a baseball game—snacks, photos with the team mascot—and even Grandpa forgetting where the car was parked after the game!

The granddaughter is old enough to remember this special event, a time when two significant people showed her how much they cared about her world.

Another grandfather noted that an approaching day off from school for his grandson would present a challenge to the working parents. He volunteered to take the boy to a local state park.

Since it was a rainy day and Grandpa discovered his grandson didn't have a good rain jacket, there was also an impromptu detour to the local sporting goods store to find a waterproof jacket. The two of them hiked the park trails, climbed a fire tower, and talked about school, life, and the boy's observations while Grandpa told some stories about outdoor trips he'd taken in various places of the world. It was memorable day for both of them, thanks to a school district and Grandpa's flexible schedule.

By making time, you can remind your grandkids that there are worthwhile, memory-building pursuits that don't happen in a hurry: chess, reading, just sitting and talking, evening walks, breakfast out on Saturday mornings, or sitting on the porch swing and watching the sunset.

Do little things

Some of the best grandfathering is expressed by thoughtful gestures that tell your grandkids in subtle ways how much you think of them.

By little things, I mean cards and letters you send, maybe with a newspaper clipping or a small trinket that made you think of your grandchild. When you travel or visit, do you find something special and personal (not necessarily costly) to give each grandchild that reflects his or her interests?

I know grandparents who put together a Christmas stocking for each grandchild, filled with little gifts that are personal to them. All year long, Grandma and Grandpa are collecting tokens that remind them of particular grandchildren and storing them for the stockings.

There are hundreds of little ways to communicate, "You're special to me." Consistently recognize your grandchild for good grades, or the ways she is showing her personal character. Reward her just for being the great kid that she is. Send an e-mail or text to see how her day is going.

Have your grandchildren school you on the latest in social media—because new apps come out almost every week—so you can literally step into their world and allow them to tell you what they are thinking about, learning, and experiencing.

Inspire and motivate

Your grandchildren will succeed in many ways, but they will also fail. They'll need comfort, sometimes advice, and always someone to be positive and believe in them, no matter what. Grandfathers are in a unique position to do just that.

Your granddaughter needs to hear your voice encouraging her by name from the stands, even if she isn't a super athlete. Your grandson will notice you in the audience at a concert, supporting his efforts.

You can be a consistent, long-term source of encouragement through all the changes that come with growing up. The point isn't trying to make your grandchildren stars, but helping them be the best they can, whatever they are pursuing.

When you're in your grandchildren's lives, they can open the door into other kids' lives whose grandparents can't be there or haven't shown an interest. Tell your grandkids you're interested in their friends because you're happy to be a grandpa to a friend who doesn't have one.

You will be offering your grandkids a golden opportunity to care for others. To do these things, you must be in their world.

Transmit values

We can transmit values when we step into the environments where our grandchildren live each day.

The world in which they are growing up probably has different—or at least changing—definitions for concepts such as family, commitment, sacrifice, respect, honesty, responsibility, work, faith, and even love.

By being in their world, you have the chance to help them see the counterfeits or distortions they will have to navigate. Believe me, this exercise will stretch you.

When you enter you grandkid's world, you're a guest. Remember that. The more you act like a guest, the more often you will be invited in. And please note that *different* and *wrong* aren't always the same! Just because something is jarring and unfamiliar doesn't necessarily make it wrong.

Take, for example, the music your grandkids think is amazing. Your initial reaction may honestly be "You call that music?" Keep that thought to yourself for the time being. It might help to remember what your parents and grandparents thought of your music!

Get beyond the music's *style* and talk about the music's *message*. What's the song really about? Is the way it's talking about other people the way we think about each other?

Choose a particular significant term in the song and ask, "When the song talks about love/honesty/commitment, what is it saying or how is it using those words?"

When you are in their world, let them be your teacher and guide. You may observe many things that upset or concern you, but before you will get a hearing from your grandkids, work at being a listener.

Much of the technology in your grandchildren's world may seem mind-boggling to you, but do your best to learn about it. Appreciate its benefits before you start criticizing its limitations.

You may want to tell your grandchildren that they spend too much time on the phone, but if some of that time is spent contacting you with little updates from their lives, your concerns may have to be softened. If your granddaughter takes an hour to walk you through the mysteries of Snapchatting, she has practically rolled out the red carpet for you to spend time in her world.

Passing on values can be one of your grandest roles as a granddad, but it's severely limited if you're not around. A granddaughter will often feel pressure to behave, or feel caught in an ongoing power struggle with her mom and dad. But with you, she can relax. She may listen more closely and ask more thoughtful questions, such as the following:

"Grandpa, when Daddy was seven, was he like me?"

"Did he have to clean up his plate?"

Or maybe, "Why did Aunt Julie get a divorce?"

She's trying to learn about her world, including her school, her family, and relationships in general. You may have a unique opportunity to help shape her young mind. You may also get a chance to support her parents by pointing out all they do for her, as well as reinforcing their established limits and routines.

In fact, it is crucial that you never put yourself between your grandkids and your kids by undermining their authority in their children's lives. If you are really concerned about something, approach Mom and Dad. Any statements to your grandkids about their parents need to be wise, measured, and at all times supportive.

The Extra Mile

Traveling and sharing with dads and granddads around the country, I hear my share of heartwarming stories and of difficult ones, too. Not everyone is able to tackle the fatherhood or grandfatherhood job with a clean slate.

Life is messy, and grandfathers should have the experience to know that's true and the willingness to step into the gaps when things fall apart. Sometimes you will need to be the rock that doesn't move when the floods of life rage.

A few years ago, a nine-year-old named Jordan wrote this about his grandpa for one of the National Center for Fathering essay contests:

Four months before I was born, my real father left my mommy. My Grandpa drove 400 miles to come get my mommy. He took care of her until I was born. When I came home from the hospital, there was a cradle that Grandpa made just for me. Someday, my kids will sleep in the same cradle.

When I was a baby, I cried a lot at night. Grandpa would walk me around and around the kitchen table. He rocked me to sleep and he was my first baby-sitter. Now I'm nine years old and Grandpa is my best buddy. We do lots of things together. We go to zoos, museums, and parks. We watch baseball games on TV and we have Chex Mix together, just the two of us.

When I was four, my Grandpa spent a whole summer building me a playhouse with a big sandbox underneath. He made me a tire swing and pushes me lots of times in it. He pushes me real high, way up over his head. Now he spends all his extra time building new rooms on our house so that Mommy and I will have our own apartment.

My Grandpa is really patient. When he is busy building things, he always takes time to start a nail so that I can pound it in. After he's spent all day mowing our big lawn he is really tired, but he will still hook my wagon up to the lawn mower and drive me all over the place.

Sometimes people on TV talk about kids from single-parent families. I'm not one of them because I have three parents in my family. My grandpa isn't my father, but I wouldn't trade him for all the dads in the world.[4]

As a dedicated grandfather, you have much to offer children in need. With the number of broken homes in our society, chances are good that you'll find that child in your own extended family. But even if you don't, there's still much you can give to other single-parent families or abandoned children, or to a family whose grandparents live far away. All of your grandfatherly assets can apply to children outside your family as well.

Granddad, building a lasting legacy is about investing in

relationships with those who will be the leaders of the next generation—your children and grandchildren. They represent your greatest legacy, and one of your most significant contributions to the future. But all of this isn't going to happen from a distance. Find some ways to enter their world and stick around for when they need you.

Inside Their World
Remember that when you step into a grandchild's world, you are also stepping into your child's world.

The following story illustrates how grandparents still have a chance to gently influence their own offspring as well as their grandchildren.

Colin is eleven and loves tennis. Not long ago his grandparents were visiting, and they asked if they could watch him play. They had heard he was making progress and wanted to encourage him. So Colin and his dad, Brian, grabbed their racquets and took Grandma and Grandpa to the high school tennis courts for an exhibition match.

Later, when Colin was off somewhere else, Brian talked to his father about their tennis excursion. He said, "Yeah, Colin isn't a natural or anything, but he's getting better. And he likes the sport. If he works hard, he could be pretty good."

His dad's response surprised him. That grandpa laid some wisdom on his son, saying, "Yes, but the best thing is that tennis is something the two of you can do together."

That's a good word for all of us dads and granddads. We need balance. If we do things only "for our kids" and not "with our kids," we're missing out on some wonderful personal benefits. Sitting by the tennis courts that day, those grandparents were multitasking, doing something with and for two generations.

Now, it's certainly good to help children excel in different areas of life—sports, hobbies, music, and the arts. They develop valuable skills and learn life lessons they may not get any other way. Spending time and resources to help kids excel at something is a good investment.

And if they have one-in-a-million talent and dedication, they might make the U.S. Open, play at Carnegie Hall, write a bestseller, grab a gold medal, or reach some other high level of achievement. Maybe they will spread the gospel to thousands or help build God's Kingdom in some amazing, unexpected ways. Chasing dreams is one of life's great joys.

But even as they dream—and you dream—don't lose perspective. Remember that the biggest benefit you can bring to their lives is your presence—just being there, being involved. That strong relationship will give them the confidence and the security to pursue whatever they do in life without having to worry about what you think about them, or why you weren't there for this or that.

That perspective will also help you be a better dad and granddad. You don't have to be overly concerned about whether your grandchild makes first team or first chair. You don't have to yell at the referees or coaches; you don't have to get uptight when you're practicing with your grandchild or watching him perform. You can apply less pressure and give more encouragement.

Best of all, you can simply enjoy spending time with your grandchild, learning about his or her world. This exploring phase of life is a great time for granddads. So, I'll see you at the ballpark!

Action Steps

1. How are you entering into your grandchild's world? The more grandkids you have and the older they become, the more worlds you'll have to juggle. (Mental and physical exercise is good for you!) As you work on your grandkids' profiles in your family tree notebook, write a brief description of the way you think each grandchild sees the world right now. Make it a point to keep working on your notebook at least once a week, compiling significant data on those grandkids and your own past.

2. Below are additional ways to enter into your grandchildren's worlds. Not all of these suggestions will work for every grandkid, but don't give up. When they remember their childhood, make it easy for them to see you in their mental pictures.

   - Make some time this week for each of your grandkids. Spread it out and don't overdo it, but include them all in your plans.
   - After each visit or activity, take a few minutes with your family tree and grandkid profiles, noting what you observed about that child.
   - Send cards and letters, newspaper clippings, e-mails, or text messages to remind your grandchildren that you're thinking of them.

- Set up a reading reward system for your grand-children based on a list of books that you choose and purchase for them.
- Explore the possibility of volunteering to read in their classroom. Or tell your grandkids, "If you ever need a show-and-tell for school, think about taking me."

CHAPTER FOUR

611: SHOW THEM YOUR WORLD

THE NUMBER 611 isn't an emergency code or a date in history. It's a locomotive number—a very famous locomotive number. You probably wouldn't discover this in your first conversation with me, but eventually the subject of trains would come up, and then you and I would travel down the tracks a little way.

Railroading is in my blood. At least two of my ancestors were railroad men. I was raised near Roanoke, Virginia, where trains, tracks, and rail schedules were part of everyday life.

Even when I'm in a hurry and I'm stuck at a train crossing, I never get upset. I'm like a kid whose bus was delayed by a circus parade on the way to school. And when I hear a train whistle blow, well, it stops me in my tracks.

Engine 611 is a huge, coal-burning, steam-driven monster of iron and steel that seems alive to me. It has a distinct baritone whistle that is more like a deep, extended hoot, and it vibrates through your soul. I would recognize it anywhere.

This locomotive was one of the "J" series of engines designed and built by Norfolk and Western employees during and after World War II up to 1950. Fourteen of these locomotives were proudly built. In a railroad age that was changing from steam to diesel power, the powerful J series engines were among the last and best of their class. They could pull trains at speeds exceeding one hundred miles per hour.

Today, only the rugged and beautiful 611 remains as a working version of those great machines. It is the crown jewel of the Virginia Transportation Museum, where it runs during special summer excursions for those who still enjoy the sound and motion of running on rails under steam power.

My children and grandchildren are learning all about number 611 because it's a window into Grandpa's world and one place they can begin to discover our family's heritage that belongs to them. They need to know that not-too-distant ancestors lived in a world where fast travel on land was strictly by rail.

When I take them to a railroad museum, they can stand next to a locomotive with wheels as tall as their daddy and experience a reality that can't be grasped from photographs. And I know they won't forget standing near the tracks when a train comes by and the ground shakes while the wind of its passing pushes us back.

By the way, trains still run all over this country. I know

one family from the Chicago area who was planning a trip to Denver, Colorado, for a larger family reunion. The grandparents decided it would be fun to travel with their children and grandchildren on a train. None of these kids had ever been on a train. The experience of traveling but being able to move about, change seats, visit the scenic car, the café, the dining car, and the bathroom was memorable. For the grandparents, it was an unforgettable delight to watch the grandkids having such fun.

Trains may not be part of your world, but you have your own story to tell. Your grandchildren deserve to know it. Find a way to let your grandchildren into your world.

Remember Your World

Do you think about your childhood games and fun times? Depending on where you grew up, there may have been local traditional games or particular rules for common games that are worth remembering and passing on.

Perhaps marbles were used in an unusual way in your neighborhood. Are you one of those city kids with vivid memories of games played with friends in the street because it was the only open space, and everyone kept an eye out for cars?

Have you told your stories? Do you still have a few of those marbles put away somewhere? Your interests and hobbies may be the key that unlocks a point of connection with your grandchild.

Find the magic and mystery of a pocketknife, pocket watch, or almost any device today's kids have never seen—like a real slingshot. Bring to life those traits that make you the granddad that you are.

I know a family of several avid deer hunters. On numerous occasions, Grandpa's kitchen has been the location for butchering the game after a successful hunt. The big table is covered in plastic and half the deer is laid out for several knife-wielding family members to go to work on.

There's something endearing about a granddaughter standing on a chair, watching the proceedings as a section of venison is cut up, asking questions about why certain parts are kept whole and others chopped for making sausage, or picking up a leg bone to feel the weight.

When she was very young and first introduced to this process, she quickly learned a response that was her role during the family activity. When Grandpa or Daddy would ask, "So, what does deer taste like?" she would smile and say with great gusto, "Delicious!"

This was a way for her to be part of the larger life of her family, and she felt welcomed and praised for her interest. The day might come when the deer on the table will be one she shot and field dressed, and she will be providing food for the family to enjoy.

What gets passed from generation to generation is sometimes more than knowledge; it's responsibility and contribution to everyone's well-being.

Part of the purpose of inviting your grandkids into your world is to show them you were like them at one time and can understand certain experiences they are having. Another reason is to show them how different things were in the world when you grew up. Maybe you had chores to do every day, or you walked to school two miles, uphill, both ways.

Don't think that giving the kids a general description of what you did will get the job done. If you say, "I helped my dad milk the cows every evening," they won't understand half of what you said.

Describe how much bigger the cows were than you were at that age. Were you using a milking parlor or were you milking by hand? Relive the moments with them so they feel like they can smell the hay and feel the ground move a little when the cows stomp their feet. Better yet, tell stories like this if at all possible, on location—in the barn where you spent time.

Perhaps there are duties you had quite young that taught you valuable lessons. As a boy, one grandfather worked for a neighbor who had some physical disabilities. He was hired during the summer to do odd jobs around the house that were hard for the man to do.

Years later, this grandfather realized the neighbor had also been schooling him on how to handle money. When he paid the boy, he talked to him about what he was going to do with all the cash he was earning. It wasn't much money, but the man schooled him on managing it with wisdom that guided not only the boy, but also the man he became, changing the financial future of his own kids and grandkids.

Your grandkids should know where and how you learned all the things you know. It will encourage them when they face challenges in school and life to know that even Grandpa didn't know some of these things when he was young.

It can be a lot of fun to serve as a living library for your grandchildren. There's a saying: "When an elderly person dies, a library burns down." Grandchildren are going to discover Wikipedia soon enough, but when the past comes with your voice and personal experiences, it will mean something different and make more of an impact in their lives.

We may think we don't know all that much, but to those little ones we are a fount of knowledge! You may also be an expert in a few things and will be able to answer some crucial questions they might have someday.

Your grandchildren need a sense of family history, and that can come from you. They need to hear your stories about your grandparents and other extended family members, about what your sons and daughters (their parents) were like, about that old Chevy you used to drive, about "the good ol' days."

When you tell stories about aunts and uncles, cousins and grandmas, you say to them, "You are part of this family." They are learning about your world as they figure out how they are part of it.

Do you ever feel kids don't appreciate their elders enough? I know what some kids think when their parents tell them the family's going over to Aunt Elsie's house: "It's boring over there." "There's nothing to do." Or they think Uncle Carl is totally out of touch.

Even so, I believe one of the best things you can do is get those extended family members together and then ask questions about the past. What was life like when they were your granddaughter's age? Did they have hobbies? Or pets? What was his first job? Did he serve in the military? How did they fall in love? What was Christmas like growing up?

When our kids were young, many times at Christmas we'd catch them soaking in all kinds of stories as their grandparents and other relatives talked about old times. I firmly believe my kids are stronger because they heard these stories. I remember as a kid myself the profound sense of comfort and rightness in watching my father sitting with friends of his, talking for hours. I often didn't understand what they were talking about, but the warmth of their shared laughter and companionship touched me.

My daughter Patrice told me about the last time she spoke to her grandma as she headed back to school. My mother told Patrice something that has stuck with her ever since: "Patrice, I'm depending on you."

My daughter told me later, "I would hear Grandmother's voice when I'd be taking a test or studying or going through some other challenge: 'I'm depending on you.'"

Grandpa, as your grandchildren grow a little older, speaking into their lives will be a privilege worth careful consideration.

Share Your Adventure

Many kids love to climb trees. My son Chance has enjoyed his tree-climbing adventures in our yard since he was young. My friend Neil has been climbing trees as long as he can remember.

He's climbed trees in Mexico, Brazil, the United States, and a few other places along the way. When his kids were young, they helped Neil build a tree house they still talk about.

As an adult, Neil added rock climbing to his tree-climbing

interests, investing in ropes and all the equipment necessary to engage in the sport while minimizing the danger of breaking his neck. If you're not familiar with rock climbing, it involves the use of hands, fingers, toes, feet, and sometimes even other body parts to ascend rock faces of various heights.

Most rock climbing is done with a safety rope attached, usually much higher than the climber, so a fall means releasing the holds and being "caught" by the rope that is controlled by a partner or "belayer."

This sounds rather matter-of-fact until you're clutching a thin ledge forty or fifty feet off the ground and realize you have no place to go or the strength left to go there—even if there was a place to put your feet. Letting go and trusting the rope and your partner is a big deal.

One of the skills to master in rock climbing is a technique called rappelling. This involves having a rope tied to an anchor point at the top of a cliff and threading the rope through a braking device attached to a harness the climber wears. The loose end of the rope then goes around the climber's waist and is controlled by his or her hand.

At this point, the climber is standing with his heels over the edge of a sheer rock face with nothing but air behind him. The only thing keeping him from falling is the rope.

Neil has photographs of the time he introduced each of his three children to rock climbing. They were still in diapers! Each of them had the thrill of doing a short rappel strapped to Dad as they descended the rope together. They took to climbing like little mountain goats and have grown up sport climbing in gyms and outdoors.

Neil has now had the privilege of introducing his five

grandchildren to rock climbing. Alongside their fathers, he's teaching them the knots they need to know, the basic safe practices of climbing, and the joy of figuring out a way to get up the cliff.

He isn't able to climb as difficult routes as he did when he was younger, but the enjoyment of the sport and the privilege of being the expert belayer to protect his precious grandkids keep Neil smiling and laughing out loud.

What I just described may be as far from your interests as you can imagine. But I'm going to guess there's an adventurous part of your life somewhere.

Maybe you collect stamps because they give you a sense of the world out there. Or perhaps you have an interest in some kind of ancient artifacts or collection of items that hold special significance for you.

One grandfather grew up flying kites and model airplanes and is now adjusting to life with a son and grandson who are fascinated by small drones. It's all about the thrill of flight.

Dangerous Stuff

Grandpa, when you and I start telling stories about our childhood, one thought behind the stories is often this: "How on earth did we live to tell about it?"

Now that we can look back at the jumping, riding, swinging, and exploring, we can see how hazardous they may have been, but it didn't feel that way at the time.

The fact is, give a boy almost any set of circumstances and he can find a way to transform it into a dangerous situation. Did we break legs and arms—get cuts, blisters, and bruises? Yes. We may even have the scars to prove it.

But we weren't trying to hurt ourselves. We were simply seeking adventure and fun. There's a special connection you can make with your grandsons and granddaughters in sharing those adventures, while not necessarily encouraging them to try the same thing when they get home.

And while we're thinking about dangerous stuff, stop and think about automobile travel when you were young. Remember those days? The back seat or the entire back section of a station wagon was the traveling activity center for the kids. You could move around.

We've taken safety to such an exaggerated level today that our vehicles can't leave the driveway without everyone buckled into an immovable, uncomfortable position. Believe me, I'm all for safety and would never want any of my precious grandchildren to be hurt. But we also live in a world where being absolutely safety conscious doesn't *guarantee* everyone will be safe.

Let me encourage you to keep your horizons broad and your sense of God's protection alive. The world is a dangerous place, but full of adventures and discoveries if we accept the fact that no amount of care, fear, or avoidance can keep us entirely safe.

Painful Memories

Some of us live with some history that's easy to remember but hard to share with others. Maybe the greatest and most terrifying adventure of your life was war—something you desperately hope your grandchildren never have to experience.

Children and grandchildren need to understand you were

protecting a way of life for them, even though they might not have been born yet.

I know one grandfather who gradually shared with his grandkids his experience as a Higgins boat driver in the Pacific theatre during World War II. Those boats were the flat-front troop carriers that took soldiers from the ships and brought them into the beaches during an attack.

Higgins boats had a metal bow that swung down to serve as a ramp when the boat reached shore so the soldiers could run out, usually while the enemy was doing everything they could to kill them. To steer the boat, the driver had to sit in an elevated position where he was a target during the trip to and from the beach.

That quiet grandfather managed to share with his children, grandchildren, and great-grandchildren the fears he had felt, the sadness in the suffering and loss he had witnessed, but also the deep sense of pride he felt in safeguarding his family's future.

He said enough to let his family know he was there, and he kept to himself enough to make the point he was still protecting them, even from the gruesome details of that sacrifice.

Your Inner World

Research indicates that the way a grandfather speaks about and lives out his faith or lack of faith has a compelling impact on his grandchildren.[1]

My personal observation is that kids can tell the difference between an authentic expression of faith in their family's life and behavior carried out for their benefit that is meaningless to the adults.

They may not understand until they are older, or until they ask, why some things are important to Grandpa, but they'll sense it. They may imitate you in ways that will surprise you.

Now, none of us is consistent in our faith or perfect in performance. Our little kids may think we walk on water, but eventually they will discover that we're just like Peter, sometimes going down in the waves of life and desperately needing Jesus' help.

But isn't that really the kind of faith we want to pass on to succeeding generations? It has to be more than just a label taken from the church we attend ("Everybody in our family is a Baptist, or Catholic, or Lutheran"). If it's not a faith that sustains us, we may still pass it on, but it won't be of real value in the lives of those who come after us.

One important part of my life is my Carolina room, a room in our house painted that wonderful shade of blue, in honor of the place I went to school, played football, and met my bride. There's a couch and TV in there, as well as plenty of other memorabilia and special photos from my six decades on this earth.

That's also where my "altar" is. I call it that, but it's really just a small table where I keep my Bible, my prayer journal, other devotionals, and what I might call "reminders" or "prayer prompters." It's where I have my quiet time and where Chance and I used to read our daily chapter from Proverbs until he left for college.

Now, I don't want to make a big deal about my "prayer altar." I definitely don't want to come across as if I'm praying on the street corner so everyone can see me—something

Jesus warns against in Matthew 6. But I occasionally mention to people that their name or picture is there on my altar as a reminder to pray for them. I hope that's an encouragement to them.

And of course, my family members know about it. My children and their spouses are used to it by now. Their attitude is, "Yeah, that's just what Dad does."

My grandkids know their pictures are in the Carolina room, and sometimes they want to look at them. And we'll look through other photos of friends, my staff, and so on.

The other day we had a bunch of grandkids over—five or six of them. When they're all together, they'll go around like a big gang, seeing what fun and mischievous things they can get into. It's a riot.

They were moving through the house and I was watching them. At one point, my oldest granddaughter, the leader of the gang, pointed to the Carolina room and said to the others, "We need to go in there and pray."

Even if they don't quite understand what that means, they know their granddad prays and that praying is a good thing to do. If there was one thing I would want my grandchildren to remember about Pi-Pa, it is that he prayed for them.

I'm reminded of Job in the Old Testament, one of the earliest men of faith in the Bible. He's described as mature, upright, and God-fearing, but when the details are filled in, the example given is that he prayed for his kids. He was concerned about their walk with God and talked to God about his concerns daily.

So let me encourage you, dad and granddad, to pray for

your kids and their kids. And pray with them. Maybe even establish your own prayer corner.

Like I said, don't do it just to be noticed. But at the same time, we shouldn't hide our prayer habit from our children. We're important models, and they need to see us living out our faith every day. When we show them our world, they need to see how God fits into it.

Once you begin to think about it, you should be able to come up with numerous ways you can invite your grandkids into your life.

Believe me, they won't get tired of hearing you say, "When I was your age . . ." They may express shock at first ("You were a kid once, Grandpa?"), but once they realize you have memories of life from their perspective, you will be amazed at the questions that might come up:

"Did you ever learn to ride a bike?"

"Did your dad ever spank you?"

"What's a telegram, Grandpa?"

You'll probably spend most of the time explaining antiques like landlines, letters, eight-track tapes, cassettes, huge TV boxes with small screens, and other details of life that are long gone.

But the best thing to let them know—again and again as you invite them into your life—is that you're very glad they are part of it.

Action Steps

1. In your family notebook, list childhood stories you want to share with your grandkids. Having the list at hand when the kids visit will keep you from having

to think on the fly. Don't worry if you tell the same story more than once. New details will emerge, and the kids will tease you about the repetition ("Pi-Pa, you told us that story before—like twenty times!"). But just as your grandkids like to hear children's books repeatedly, they'll like to hear your stories over and over too.

2. How do you pray for each of your grandkids? One of the benefits of developing a profile for each of them is that in the process you will see matters you should pray about. If your granddaughter wants to be a nurse or doctor, she has a long road of training ahead that you can pray over. It's easy to promise to pray for a grandchild when you hold that baby in the hospital, but it joins the other promises in your life (like your wedding vows) that require a daily practice. Praying for your grandchildren regularly is one way you make them part of your life.

3. At the very least, have a page of prayer points that relate to each grandkid. From time to time, remind your grandkids that you pray for them and ask them for prayer requests.

4. Many people have "bucket lists" of things they want to do in their lifetime. Why don't you also start a "dump the bucket list" of your past adventures and experiences you want to tell your grandkids about?

Add stories to the list as they come to mind, and refer to the list from time to time. That way, you'll be ready when occasions arise that provide a perfect setting for the story.

CHAPTER FIVE

CHANGING YOUR GRANDKIDS' HERITAGE

THE WORDS *HERITAGE* and *legacy* are often used interchangeably in conversation, but they are not the same thing.

Heritage is the combined traditions, beliefs, behaviors, achievements, and failures that your ancestors have passed along to you. You can't change it.

Legacy is what you add to your heritage before you pass it on to your children and grandchildren. *That* you can control a great deal.

The past is sealed in time; your present is unfolding and it will alter the heritage of your children and grandchildren. Your legacy is the one part of your descendants' heritage that you can change.

Death is the dividing line between heritage and legacy.

The people alive in your family right now are creating legacies each day as they deal with their heritage and interact with the rest of the family.

This process is an intricate weaving of lives that God has designed for His purposes. For better or for worse, those in the grave have made their contribution. Those walking around have choices to make about their heritage.

Until you take your last breath, you have the opportunity to make an impact on your descendants by leaving them *your* legacy.

Here's the point: Your heritage has been defined by others. It has benefits, limits, and liabilities.

But your legacy remains undefined. It has no limits. It only has potential. How you handle your heritage and what you add to it as your legacy will change or confirm the heritage of your children and grandchildren.

The main reason it's important to know about your own heritage (and introduce your kids and grandkids to theirs) is that while you can't change it, you can decide how to respond to it.

You can simply choose to continue certain traditions or behaviors, or reject them and establish different ones. Your legacy is then reversing or altering the direction of heritage for those who come after you. This can have both negative and positive effects for generations to come.

If your father and grandfather had issues with alcohol, it's likely a recurring problem in your heritage. When you realize this, you have some important decisions to make about your own life—decisions that may make a huge difference for your kids and grandkids.

Let's say there is a history of unbelief and resistance to God in your family and you become the first person to trust Christ. You won't be changing the past, but your decision will impact your own eternal destiny and that of your descendants.

Vern Bengtson and his associates have been tracking more than 350 families across four generations now spanning a period of fifty years. Their recent book, *Families and Faith: How Religion Is Passed Down across Generations,* resulted from those studies.

The title of the fifth chapter in Bengtson's book caught my attention: "The Unexpected Importance of Grandparents and Great-Grandparents." This research team has noted a remarkable consistency in the influence of grandfathers on their grandchildren, often in cases where the same influence doesn't seem to have affected their own children.[1]

People may grow up and reject their parents' faith, for example, yet witness their own children reverse that choice and follow the pattern of their grandparents. This research offers hope that grandparents may be able to significantly help their grandchildren.

In God's design, parents are the main delivery system for the heritage they have received. Parents create legacy, including the living legacy that is their children.

As a grandparent, you can be much more of an intentional conduit between the heritage you are about to become and the lives of your grandchildren. You are in the best position to consider and act on what transpired in your family leading up to you, and what will happen after you're gone.

In the six years since *Championship Fathering* was

published, I've become even more convinced of the following thoughts:

> I've gotten to know a number of men whose heritage was nothing short of a handicap. Their fathers and grandfathers didn't seem to care what kind of legacy they were passing on. But I've seen these men take on the challenge of making things different for their own children. I've watched them day by day, patiently taking sad and shameful heritages and creating legacies that would make their children proud and healthy adults. For your kids' sake, don't get so hung up on your heritage that you fail to shape your legacy.[2]

At the time, I was thinking mostly about the fathering role, but I knew I had to include grandfathers. Now I realize that my role in my grandchildren's lives is a crucial part of the heritage they will receive. I can change their heritage by what I do.

Thinking Biblically

According to one proverb in the Bible, "Children's children are the crown of old men" (Proverbs 17:6, NKJV). Just think about that picture for a minute. Crowns are often adorned with valuable gems. Didn't it seem as if a jewel was added to your life the moment you discovered you were a grandfather?

Even if I don't wear a physical crown with a precious stone representing each of my grandkids, those little ones are always on my mind. Yes, they are my crown, shining right now with nine living statements that Carey Casey lived on Earth.

Grandfathers should have a keen sense that they are leaving a legacy, and that awareness can be motivating and energizing.

Consider this: Did you ever meet your great-grandparents? Do you even know the names of your great-grandfather or great-grandmother? If you've been working on your family tree, you should. I hope you are feeling more and more connected with those whose lives have shaped yours.

But I suspect many reading these words don't know their great-grandparents' names, not to mention what they did with their lives, what they stood for, and what they believed in.

Now that may not seem like a big deal, but think of it this way: Will your great-grandchildren know *your* name? If the trend holds true, probably not. So we may well be three or four generations from being completely forgotten!

I don't know about you, but I want to leave a better, more lasting legacy than that—not because I want my descendants to remember how great I was or how much I accomplished. I'm not talking about running for senator or building a world-famous business. No, I want to be remembered as just one of many in a long line who built a reputation of high character, a close-knit family, and a deep faith in Christ. That's what it's all about!

If you're thinking as you read this that it's too late for you, you're wrong. Grandfather, no matter what you may have been through in your past and how you've built your legacy to this moment, you can turn things around for your descendants yet to come by being faithful to God and humbly serving your family.

It isn't just about what you can do differently; it's mostly about realizing that God can do something amazing in your life, just as He did in Dr. John Perkins' life.

A New Legacy

Here's a brief history of a great man—Dr. John Perkins. He grew up on a plantation, as a poor sharecropper's son who dropped out of school after the third grade.

He'll tell you that he came from a family with a less-than-spotless reputation. Back then, the Perkins family name was associated with bootlegging and gambling.

Dr. Perkins grew up and came to know Christ, and became a leading voice for civil rights. He is a highly respected author and speaker on topics such as racial reconciliation, the importance of faith and education, community development, and leadership. This man with a third-grade education has honorary doctorates from nine colleges! He's also active in several ministries and foundations focused on serving the poor and bringing hope to desperate communities.

Why the history lesson? It just so happens that my daughter Patrice married Dr. Perkins' grandson, also named John. Marriage brings two people, two families, and two family trees together. All of a sudden, there's a new collection of stories to learn.

My son-in-law found one of his family's stories in a book about African American heroes. Flipping through it, he saw stories about Mary McLeod Bethune, Harriet Tubman, and

Martin Luther King. Then he turned the page and found a story about his grandfather, Dr. Perkins.

A day or so after my second grandchild was born to John and Patrice, I witnessed something inspiring. I saw John, the baby's daddy, reading from that book about *his* granddaddy to Dr. Perkins' great-grandson.

And no one had to tell him to do that. He was expressing his father's heart, thinking about his own heritage and wanting to pass that on as part of his legacy. What a great blessing!

I had the privilege of talking to Dr. Perkins on the phone, celebrating this new addition to our family. His natural response was to praise God. Thinking about his own upbringing and his family's bad reputation, he commented, "Now my legacy has changed, Carey."

That's the grace of God and an example of the Championship Fathering and Championship Grandfathering culture we're encouraging here at the National Center for Fathering. I trust you sense a renewed or growing desire to see what God can do in your life.

Handling Your Heritage

One undeniable truth about fathering is that the present and the future are linked to the past. Though we might not like to admit it, upon reflection, most of us can see qualities of our fathers in ourselves.

And if we are blessed with grandchildren, there's a good chance we'll see some of our father's qualities as well as our own traits repeated in the way our children parent their kids. Of course, they would never admit to that.

My kids used to make fun of me for being like my dad,

and now I see them doing some of the same things I did! As I hear my children saying phrases to their children that my bride and I have used, I smile at the echo.

Sometimes these repetitions are actually intentional. One grandfather I know had two standard answers for those times during long automobile rides when his kids would ask, "When are we getting there?"

The first answer came with a straight face: "In twelve days."

When the children were older and no longer accepted that answer, his fallback reply was, "Well, every time the wheels go around we get a little closer."

Imagine that dad's joy the first time he heard one of his sons answer his own little daughter's predictable travel question with that famous answer: "In twelve days." He laughed out loud!

That's a lighthearted example, but sometimes what is repeated in you or in your children isn't funny. Who wants to pass on destructive habits, uncontrolled anger, irresponsibility, or absence?

Many times, when we become fathers and grandfathers, we start processing the past and begin planning for the future— for our children and future grandchildren. It takes humility to realize you are repeating a bad habit you don't want to pass on. Realizing how you ended up with a trait is an explanation; it's not an excuse to keep repeating that behavior.

One grandfather I talked to remembers how his own father had a habit of raising his voice when he answered his wife's questions. His tone communicated impatience and sometimes anger.

His son realized he was doing the same thing with his wife and decided that wasn't going to be a pattern any more. But it has taken a long time to break that habit, and he admits that under certain circumstances, he still hears his voice increasing in volume unnecessarily. He's fortunate to have a patient and forgiving bride who is helping him put aside that way of communicating.

So then, how can you leave a positive legacy for your children and grandchildren when thinking about parts of your heritage brings mostly pain? You may not want to dwell on the past; you may think there's no point in going there.

But it's important to understand how your father and grandfathers have influenced you—whether it's mostly positive or even if it's negative—so you can learn from it and gain a sense of purpose as you seek to be the father and grandfather your family needs.

Understanding your heritage is a complicated process, but here are two important steps I'll mention briefly:

First, list those qualities that are part of your fathering heritage—the ways your father influenced you. Really reflect on them. Write them down. Ask God to reveal the difference—the positive and negative—that this heritage has made in your life.

Second, with those things in mind, begin to plan the future and be intentional about making sure your dreams for your children and grandchildren become a reality. How can you capitalize on the good you received and help your children and grandchildren avoid the bad?

It's not enough to look at our heritage and conclude, "I don't want to be like that!" Recognizing a bad habit or trait and then rejecting it is only a start, and won't help us if we don't make some significant decisions.

You see, a negative isn't a goal. It doesn't help to simply say what we *don't* want to be or do. And the statement "Anything but that!" isn't much better. To change a past wrong we must find a goal to move toward, a target to hit. If your father or grandfather had a trait you want to eliminate, what trait do you want to replace it with?

A young man watched his father and grandfather's lives disintegrate because of alcoholism. He told his pastor, "There's no way I'm going to be like that!"

The problem was he never decided what or who he was going to be *instead*, and he never clarified which choices had resulted in the destructiveness he saw so clearly in his heritage.

Because he paid attention only to the results and not the causes, he ended up repeating the mistakes of his heritage and causing the same pain for his own children. His life came under increasing control of alcohol even as he insisted he wasn't going to be like his dad and granddad.

It wasn't enough that he truly wanted a different result if he persisted in the same habits as those before him.

I'm going to share another possible outcome, but first I need to interrupt you if you are thinking of and pain-fully aware of habits and traits in your adult children that you realize were inherited from you. Recognizing this is an important step.

Repentance is a crucial next step. Sin in your life needs to be dealt with even before you attempt to address its impact on other lives. It has to be more than feeling bad or having regrets; repentance is a deep-seated rejection of the sin, followed by calling out to God for His help to change.

Confession before repentance doesn't lead to change, but when we honestly confess from a heart and mind willing to change, God listens. First John 1:9 says, "If we confess our sins, he is faithful and just and will forgive us our sins and purify us from all unrighteousness."

Once things are settled with God and you are dealing with the problem in your life, you can take the step of seeking forgiveness from your children. Encourage them to ask God for help, just as you are. They will be more likely to extend forgiveness if they see evidence of change in you.

Heritage handling almost always comes with some pain and shame. Those are the realities of living in a fallen, sinful world, and they are shared by everyone. The details in your heritage, good or bad, don't matter as much as what you do about them.

It Gets Personal

My grandfather on my mother's side died when I was very young. I heard stories about his early years, when he hung out in bars and had a reputation as a heavy drinker, but I only heard them years later. Those stories surprised me.

You see, he became a Christian, and the reputation of his later life far exceeded and overshadowed his difficult past. He changed his ways, and *that's* what people remembered about him, including me.

I can see in the "closed book" of his life that the early chapters might have led him to a different ending, but God got involved and changed the expected outcome of the story.

What could have been a dark time in my heritage turned out to be a time filled with grace and the evidence that with God, there's always hope.

Action Steps

1. Consider the traits, memories, and experiences of your heritage that you don't want to transfer to the next generation. What patterns need to end with you?

2. Have you already passed on traits and habits to your descendants that you now know should be eliminated? What step can you take to begin making peace with God and then pursuing forgiveness from others?

3. It's crucial to remember, Grandpa, that you're now speaking into and living in front of at least two generations. Don't hesitate to ask for God's help.

CHAPTER SIX

BUILDING A POSITIVE LEGACY

I FEEL AS IF I HAVE just started my grandfathering journey. Actually, I know it. With nine grandchildren currently under the age of eight, my flock of little ones has exploded, and I'm learning on the run. I have an understanding of who I want to be in the lives of my children's children, but I realize I have a long way to go to build a positive legacy.

The heart of Championship Grandfathering is a deeper and lasting version of Championship Fathering. The three crucial fathering roles—loving, coaching, and modeling—need to be taken to another level for a new generation.

These fundamental roles weren't my hunches but were the result of research—thousands of questionnaires giving people a chance to think about and say what had affected their lives the most in their relationships with their fathers.

There hasn't been nearly as much research on the grandfather role, but the data suggest it's an important extension of fathering. In the next three chapters, we'll consider how a grandfather loves, coaches, and models—but with an added twist.

While a dad loves, coaches, and models for his children, a grandfather's challenge is to create a legacy of loving, a legacy of coaching, and a legacy of modeling.

I'm not downplaying in any way the significance of a father's legacy, but the around-the-clock task for dads is harder to track as it's unfolding. Grandfathers are much more aware and intentional about the legacy they are leaving behind.

I think too often we speak of legacy as a list of accomplishments. Particularly for men, it's easy to think that we'll be remembered because of our important accomplishments. But real legacy centers on patterns and relationships. Your legacy is not something great you did one time, but the significant ways you interact with others day after day for a long time.

A Healthy Model

We can't have too many good models. When you see a healthy trait or habit in someone else, acknowledge it and ask if it was developed in a specific way.

For one thing, it may be a great encouragement to that person. Most of us don't have people noticing and pointing out to us *good* things we've done. We're more used to hearing what we're doing *wrong*. But you may be offered some amazing wisdom as a result of pointing out someone else's good qualities.

I find it's a great conversation starter to say, "I noticed just now how you acted in that situation. You had a great response. Will you school me up on how you learned to do that?" It's not surprising to me anymore how often I hear, "I watched my grandfather's way of handling things and found it works for me, too."

Some of my models come from the Bible. Have you looked at Titus 2 lately? I did the other day, and it's deep! Paul was encouraging Titus to teach people in the church how to behave.

Verse 2 says: "Teach the older men to be temperate, worthy of respect, self-controlled, and sound in faith, in love and in endurance."

I am sixty now, so I guess that's for me. I'm not old— just older. So, what does Paul's checklist for Titus give me to work on?

Temperate means even-tempered and not subject to unhealthy extremes. I don't think it means that a man my age shouldn't have a temper; it means that by now I should have learned to express my temper about the right things. The scene of Jesus in the Temple clearing out the money changers and animal traders is the picture of a man expressing deep anger in a healthy and uncompromising way.

Likewise, my grandkids should see me express gladness, humor, sadness, and interest in ways that match my experience in life. The grandpas I admire the most are those who share a childlike joy with their grandchildren. Temperance also means you don't take yourself too seriously. Kids love it when you're not too "adult" to be silly with them.

Your grandchildren won't know you're temperate if you never spend time with them. Passing on this trait depends on the grandkids being with you in various situations while you set a consistent example for them. And that doesn't mean it's a flawless example.

One granddaughter clearly remembers her grandfather being accosted and patted down because airport security overheard his joke about bombs. It was an unforgettable lesson for her that didn't diminish her love for her grandfather. Let your grandkids experience as much of life with you as possible.

Worthy of respect is a standing you earn as you live your life before others with integrity and consistency. Men want to be respected, but we need to remember that while respect sometimes accompanies a position or office, genuine respect comes from the way we treat people.

The way my dad treated older men left a lasting impression on me. He had earned my respect, so when he showed respect to others, I realized I owed them double honor. He taught me to treat an older man with respect until that man proved unworthy of it.

As much as I agree that a child's view of God is deeply influenced by experiences with his or her father, I also believe that grandfathers offer early exposure to awe, wisdom, and joy that dads sometimes have a hard time offering their children.

Remembering my grandfather's laugh makes me feel warm all over. Knowing that he could laugh that way after what he faced and overcame in life simply makes my respect for him grow deeper years after his death.

The *self-controlled* man in Titus 2 describes a Christian who consistently asks God for help with control issues. This isn't about us exercising self-will and power over ourselves, but letting God work in us and with us in an amazing way.

To others it may look like we're in control, but we know the difference between when we're in charge and when God's running the show.

I know that the lasting impressions my grandfather and his friends left on me had much to do with their quiet and deliberate way of doing their business. They weren't showy or famous, but they did their work and lived their lives with dignity and excellence that modeled self-control for me.

The next term Paul mentions is *sound* as it applies to faith, love, and endurance. Being sound in these qualities doesn't mean they show up here and there in life; they are consistently seen and felt by others. Something sound has been tested.

When reality raps its knuckles on your life, the tone is solid, not an empty echo. Your faith is more than a word you use occasionally. Those closest to you see you living it out. They know your love even when they don't deserve it. And they have watched you endure.

I've mentioned that one of my dad's words of wisdom was *persevere*. Every time I hear that word, a picture of Pop comes to mind: quiet, composed, and able to endure some harsh moments with grace and even a touch of humor.

I will never forget walking next to him down the sidewalk after someone shouted a racial slur at him. He glanced down at me with one of those "you've got to feel sorry for a man like that" looks, and said, "I guess he just didn't know my name."

Paul goes on to give Titus some pointers about teaching women, and then addresses younger men. He says, "Encourage the young men to be self-controlled" (v. 6). To be an older self-controlled man, it's good to start early and keep working at it.

Self-control relates to knowing who you are and who God is. Dad loved a famous movie line used by a Clint Eastwood character: "A man's gotta know his limitations." I always had the sense that because my father knew God, he didn't have to try to be "bigger" than he was.

The older I became, the more I could see that while my dad wasn't perfect, he had amazing qualities that he used to touch other people's lives.

My father didn't have a title or a high position in the world. He was "Deacon Casey," and that did mean something. But his lasting impact resulted from his character, his reputation, and his relationships with others.

Pop understood his limitations, but he didn't let them restrict him. He worked within them. I've seen this in action in my role as CEO of the National Center for Fathering when I've been invited to speak at chapel for NFL teams.

When my dad was still alive, he occasionally traveled with me. One memorable time I was speaking at the Buffalo Bills pre-game chapel service, and I introduced Dad to Coach Marv Levy. The two of them hit it off like old friends, and I stood there feeling like a little kid.

I was struck by how immediately comfortable they were

with each other, even though their daily lives were completely different. They were men of a certain age who immediately shared a bond I appreciated, in awe, from a distance. Their mutual respect had nothing to do with fame, position, or prestige.

Following Paul's description of a godly older man's characteristics, he delivers the equivalent of a great locker room speech:

> In everything *set them an example* [emphasis mine] by doing what is good. In your teaching show integrity, seriousness and soundness of speech that cannot be condemned, so that those who oppose you may be ashamed because they have nothing bad to say about us.
>
> TITUS 2:7-8

I like the idea of being an example to younger men. I have two sons who are young men—one is about to move out of his teenage years—as well as two sons-in-law, so I take my role seriously when it comes to modeling for them and my grandchildren.

Let me encourage you, too, to strive for a great reputation, where no one has anything bad to say about you. Not that you're *hiding* your faults and sins, or showing your good side only when you're in public. But when you're living with integrity around the clock, people can't help noticing. This is one of the most influential ways to shape your grandchildren's heritage.

So Dad and Granddad, I simply want to remind you—with

Paul's help—about the power of modeling. Consider this: How will people think of you when you're gone? How will your children think of you? Have you provided any reasons for people to speak negatively about you? Your integrity matters, in public and in private, and it is part of your legacy.

Whether you consider yourself "older" or "younger," I challenge you to read those verses in Titus and see how God might be speaking to you. He just might suggest ways you can change your descendants' heritage.

Thinking in Patterns

One tool to help us be healthy models and build a positive legacy involves creating patterns. As men, we tend to think too much about single instances and not enough about patterns.

For example, we might agree that it's important for us to help our brides with jobs around the house. But when asked how we're doing with that, we're likely to say, "Well, there was that one day last month when I took out the garbage without being asked."

Or maybe you know that your bride likes to hear three certain words from you. "I'm doing fine in that department," you say, "because I distinctly recall telling her 'I love you' three years ago on a Tuesday."

I know we're not that bad or clueless (most of the time), but it's almost funny to realize how our minds work. It's easy to highlight a single occasion when we stepped up and did something the right way while overlooking the day-after-day failures that can create an unhealthy pattern of behavior.

What would your bride say your "patterns" are? Ask, "Honey what would you say are the three best and three least desirable patterns you see in me?" Here's the scary thought: She will probably be able to name them right away.

Of course it's encouraging when our bride responds positively: "These are the patterns I see in you that keep me proud to be your wife. I love the way you consistently do this or that." But we also need to be ready to hear her encouragement to *change* as well as to keep up the good work.

As grandfathers, we sometimes lean on the single-example type of thinking rather than the pattern-type of thinking in our relationships with our grandkids. Doing something *one time* with a grandchild isn't a pattern. We might remember it, but they probably won't. A *pattern* is an action repeated often enough to be noticed or remembered.

One set of grandparents I know lived overseas, so they didn't see their grandchildren as often as they would have liked. But every time they visited those grandchildren, they spent individual time with each one doing something special together.

Another couple makes it a habit to give their grandchildren a big welcome. When they hear the car in the driveway, they step out the front door (even in winter) and enthusiastically greet their favorite guests on the porch. One grandfather enjoys surprising his grandkids by fixing their favorite meals when they visit.

What I want for you and for me are patterns worth imitating. A pattern isn't perfection. Championship Fathering and Grandfathering isn't about perfection; it's about getting better by practicing perseverance in the matters that matter most—the people God has placed in our lives.

Telling God's Stories

As a Christian grandfather, I have a resource in the Bible that explains and extends my legacy to my children and grandchildren in the largest way possible. I can connect them with God in their earliest years and help them see all the ways He wants to speak into their lives.

To do that, I need to interact personally with God's Word. The Bible even includes help for grandfathers!

For example, the beginning of Psalm 78 says:

I will open my mouth in parables,
    I will utter hidden things, things from of old—
what we have heard and known,
    what our fathers have told us.
We will not hide them from their children;
    we will tell the next generation
the praiseworthy deeds of the LORD,
    his power, and the wonders he has done.
He decreed statutes for Jacob
    and established the law in Israel,
which he commanded our forefathers
    to teach their children,
so the next generation would know them,
    even the children yet to be born,
    and they in turn would tell their children.
Then they would put their trust in God

and would not forget his deeds
but would keep his commands.

PSALM 78:2-7

What a picture of how to pass on a living faith to our children and grandchildren! Amen? According to this psalm, we should include *God's* stories when we talk to them.

As it says, we should open our mouths in parables—stories that communicate a powerful lesson. We should tell our children "things from of old"—what our fathers have told us. Whatever blessings we have received from our fathers, we must pass those along to our children. We must not hide the great lessons from them.

I know you're not hiding these lessons intentionally. But Grandpa, have you made it a point to think about and identify God's work in your family history? Sometimes things seem hidden because we haven't looked for them or didn't pay careful attention when we were told about them.

Are you proactive in telling the next generation about praiseworthy deeds and wonders of the Lord?

What stories can you tell about God's intervention in your life? Think of prayers that were answered, moments of unexpected provision, small miracles that opened your eyes to His love, and experiences that demonstrated His majesty and power.

Have you talked with your children and grandchildren about these things? Do you see God working in your church, your small group, or your neighborhood? Point those things out to your family! Let them experience God's power through you.

And then, as it says, give them a vision for their own future—how someday they will tell these or similar stories to their own children. They will tell of God's wonders and pass on that legacy of faith.

Action Steps

1. What can you do this very day to build a lasting, godly legacy? Are there activities you've been meaning to do with your children and grandchildren? Or talks you've wanted to have? It's time to make them a priority—today or this weekend—because that's how we create memories and shape heritage for the next generations.

2. If you've recognized some negative patterns in your life or heritage, don't stop until you have listed or described an alternative action or pattern. If your family has a long-established pattern of dishonesty or unfaithfulness, it isn't enough to say that pattern is going to stop. You also need to complete this sentence: "To end this pattern, our family will consistently practice these traits: _____

_____

_____."

3. What are your favorite Bible stories? Why are they your favorites? Answering those two questions will give you material for several conversations with your grandkids. They need to know firsthand how God's Word affects your thinking and your life.

CHAPTER SEVEN

A LEGACY OF LOVING

BEFORE WE CAN TALK seriously about the way you *love*, Grandpa, we need to think about the ways you've *been loved*. This might be painful and hard to think about, but your experience and understanding of being loved has shaped the way you love others.

Negative examples are easy to see. Most people who abuse children were themselves abused as children. Some of the darkness you may discover in trying to understand your family tree is the presence of certain hurtful habits that have been passed from generation to generation. If that's what you've found, it's time to change those habits going forward.

It's hard to see your son or daughter displaying negative

attitudes or behaviors in the way they parent, realizing they learned those from you. Before you can tell them to stop doing what they're doing, you need to admit you passed those behaviors on to them and then apologize.

You may first have to change your own attitude or behavior before you can expect them to hear your advice. "Do as I say, not as I do" doesn't work.

I believe that you will not love better than you have been loved. Remembering firsthand the pain caused when your parents were uninvolved, abusive, or harsh sets you on a quest for love and for loving others in a better way. But to love others better than you've been loved, you must first receive genuine love from someone.

Knowing that you need to love isn't enough if you don't have a reservoir of love in your own life to draw from. The dads and granddads I know who have overcome a negative and destructive past have done so with the love God has supplied directly or indirectly.

If your dad and mom loved you well, loving your children may seem simple most of the time. Or maybe you had a grandparent or family friend who cared for you in a way that stockpiled love for others in you.

But even if your upbringing was outstanding, you still need an ongoing source of love that makes up for all those times your own love falls short. Love always comes from somewhere. It doesn't start with us. And many of us reach the age of grandfathering without learning much about the true source of love.

God loves you, Grandpa. Messed up, confused, tired, and hurt, you are still loved by God. Really. One of my favorite Bible verses is Romans 5:8: "But God demonstrates his own love for us in this: While we were still sinners, Christ died for us."

I know that sounds crazy, right? It is exactly opposite to the way we think. The more we realize how sinful we are, the more we conclude that God could never love us. Yes, God knows all about our sin, but He loves us and is willing to forgive. In fact, He is the source of love.

If the idea of loving is a mystery to you, start solving it by letting God love you. He will not only love you, but will also help you love others. The Bible also tells us, "We love because he first loved us" (1 John 4:19). It's never too late for a grandpa who's still breathing to discover the love of God.

If you're tracking with me right now, realize that older men often get to this point and then turn away because they are ashamed. They are embarrassed that they waited so long to get serious about God. It's not so much that they can't imagine God loving them; it's more that they kick themselves for being so thickheaded or hard-hearted most of their lives when they could have been living differently.

Listen—as men we don't want to ask for directions because we think we can find our own way. We keep cruising until we're completely lost because we won't admit what we know: that we have no idea where we are.

If we act that way in our relationship with God, it hurts our marriages, our children, our grandchildren, and us. When it comes to life, God's love functions like a GPS, helping you find your way through confusing situations.

The foundation of a legacy of love is God's love for you. You will be able to better love the people you want to love if you allow God to love you the way He has always wanted to love you. That kind of love is experienced in the life, the words, the Cross, and the living presence of Jesus in you.

And know this: We don't start loving God before God loves us. His love is not conditional. He doesn't say, "I won't love you until you love me." He loved us even before we existed, so our love is always catch-up love. Here's how the Bible puts it:

> This is how God showed his love among us: He sent his one and only Son into the world that we might live through him. This is love: not that we loved God, but that he loved us and sent his Son as an atoning sacrifice for our sins.
>
> I JOHN 4:9-10

The best way to begin leaving a legacy of love for your grandchildren and future generations is to earnestly tell them this: "You know what? God sure loves your grandpa. God loves me a whole lot." Tell them that you've been humbled, changed, and motivated by Jesus Christ, the greatest expression of that love.

It's not hard to tell your grandchildren, "God loves you, and I do too." But it completes the picture in a personal way when you add, "And I'm glad that God loves Grandpa, too!" Knowing you've accepted God's love can make it easier for them to accept it too.

Loving Grandma

Just in case you haven't noticed this yet, I love my bride. If you also are blessed to have your bride by your side, consider her influence on your life. Let me put it this way: If I have succeeded in any way at being a good husband, father, and grandfather, I owe much to my bride's help. Her patience, forgiveness, and creativity have made me look good more times than I can count.

She's a gifted teacher, a wonderful homemaker, and a great cook. I call her my bride because that's what she is and will always be to me. I am a blessed man. In the words of Proverbs 31:28, her children and I "rise up and call her blessed" (ESV). She makes it easy for me to love her and to show my grandkids that love.

In the chapters on love in *Championship Fathering*, I talked about loving our kids before I talked about loving our kids' mother. If I had to do it over, I might switch the order. This time, I've got my priorities straight. Loving my bride came long before my children arrived, and it continues strong as our fourth child, Chance, leaves the house for college.

During many years in our marriage, life could have gradually become just about the kids, but we've kept things going in a good way. We remember that even though we are parents and now grandparents, we're also a couple with a lot of life to share.

In your season of Championship Grandfathering, it would be wise to intentionally orchestrate moments in which your grandkids experience you and your bride doing things together with them and demonstrating your love for each other.

I have a friend in ministry who gives this advice to young couples he's marrying:

> I know you think there's nothing better than the love
> you have for each other right now, and I agree that
> it's a good thing. But it can grow into something
> even better, and it needs to. One of the main reasons
> marriage is for life is because it takes that long for
> start-up love to grow into grown-up love. What
> you have right now will get you down the aisle and
> on your way, but it needs to be fed and cared for
> to develop the strength to handle everything you
> will face in life. The love you have now is ready for
> keeping the promise of "I take you for better, for
> richer, in health, and to love," but you'll need to
> strengthen your love for the promise of "'for worse,
> for poorer, in sickness, and to cherish." That kind
> of grown-up love is worth having.

I'm glad he's letting me quote him because I know he's right. My bride is still my bride, but the love we have several decades down the road is richer, deeper, and stronger than what we had when we looked into each other's eyes at the altar. She still looks younger than I do, but we both are showing signs of mileage. It doesn't matter; she's still beautiful to me.

Surprise your bride the next time the grandkids are over by pulling out your wedding photographs and telling the family you want to share one of your favorite books with them. Tell them you can't read it to them because it only has pictures, but believe me, those pictures will tell a thousand stories.

The kids will probably giggle over the hairstyles and notice that you actually had hair back then. Be ready for all kinds of unexpected questions—they won't see those photos the way you do.

Be sure to tell them about any funny and unplanned things that happened. If your "grand gang" includes both genders, consider what might appeal to boys as well as to girls. Your granddaughters might want to hear all about the ceremony, flowers, and dresses, while the grandsons will want to know about the way you tripped on the way into the church or lost the ring.

Tell them how you felt at certain points in that day. For instance, what were you thinking the first time your bride appeared at the back of the church?

Be intentional in the way you talk about how much you loved her then and how much you love her all these years later. Embarrass her with affection. This will be an example of inviting them into your world during a significant moment in your life.

And at some point say, "If this hadn't happened, you wouldn't be here!"

I read a story recently written by a professional photographer who was hired by a middle-aged woman. This woman wanted to give her husband a special album filled with photos of herself. She instructed the photographer to touch up all the pictures, edit all the flaws, airbrush her pregnancy stretch marks, and remove the little bulges here and there that she thought made her old and ugly. She then had the pictures bound together and gave them as a gift to her husband.

The photographer later received a note from that man, complimenting her on the quality of her work but profoundly observing that as excellent as the photos were, they were not really of his wife. The "defects" the photographer had carefully removed from the photographs were the very things that made that woman his wife, lover, and life partner. Those weren't flaws to be eliminated or ugliness to be erased; they were part of the deeper beauty of his woman, his bride.

That grandfather ended his note by thanking the photographer. She helped him realize that he needed to tell his wife more often how beautiful she was to him. Have you told your bride today how beautiful she is to you? I just did, and it was worth it!

To showcase your love for your bride, find ways to spend time with her and your grandkids. When she's teaching the kids something new, join the class—you might learn something. At least sit in so the kids know you're interested, even if coloring, quilting, or knitting isn't your cup of tea.

If you're doing some "boy stuff" or competitive activity that's not Grandma's thing, consider having her be the referee or judge so she can be involved.

You might recruit the grandkids to be co-conspirators when you're doing something special for Grandma. Let them deliver notes or little gifts to her from you. The kids will see love expressed in the way you include one another and will be secure in that circle of love.

The two of you are in this for the long haul. I, for one, don't want to forget that for a moment while I'm encouraging you toward Championship Grandfathering.

Loving Kids and Grandkids

Once I asked a grandfather, "What have you found to be the biggest difference between being a dad and a granddad?

He answered almost instantly, "I love my grandkids more." I think he saw a look of shock on my face because he added, "Oh, I love my kids a lot, and I wouldn't trade any of them in for a better model, but my grandkids have opened up an outlet of love I didn't know I had in me."

I think I know what he means. That's the truth behind the tongue-in-cheek story about the grandfather who declared, "If I'd know how much fun grandkids were going to be, I would have skipped the kids and gone right to them!"

In fact, in *Championship Fathering* I wrote, "My bride and I have four children, and each gets maximum love. I've been amazed how my capacity to love has grown now that three of my children are married and I have even more 'kids' to love. Now that my grandchildren are arriving, I've got this love thing on a roll—so bring on my grandkids!"

That was six or seven grandkids ago, and it's still true. Parent and grandparent love, energized by God's love, has no bounds. It expands to hold all those under its care.

I have often thought about the unique season I've found myself in—a season that is coming to an end. I've been a grandfather during most of my son Chance's adolescent years. He has enjoyed being Uncle Chance as a teenager (most of the time), but he also wants to keep that father-son "thing" going with me and so do I.

I encourage you, Grandpa, not to give up any of your fathering opportunities as grandfathering becomes a bigger part of your life.

When I'm speaking with fathers, it doesn't surprise me anymore how often I hear: "I don't understand it, Case. My dad says all these amazing things to my children that he never said to me—like 'I love you.'"

Your son might tell me this, Grandpa, but he probably won't tell you. It's too hard, and he doesn't know how—just like you didn't know how to say certain things to him when he was growing up.

Someone has to step up and open the line of communication. One of you has to go where you haven't gone before and talk about your importance to each other. And as Dad, you should lead the way.

Treating your son like a man is important, and he needs that too, but he still needs to hear statements from you that begin with the word *son*. He wants you to affirm what he is doing as a man, but he also doesn't want you to forget you are his father.

Of course, I'm not leaving daughters and granddaughters out of this picture. As you watch your son(s) and grandson(s) grow up to be men like you, you're also watching your daughter(s) and granddaughter(s) grow up into someone not like you. That doesn't matter; they still need you as their father and grandfather. The way you value, honor, and treat your daughter and granddaughter will make a huge difference in how they see themselves.

For better or for worse, the way you speak into your daughter's and granddaughter's lives will shape in many ways how they respond to men. Don't leave them to find from other men the worth, acceptance, and sense of inner beauty that should come from you as the first man (or back-up man) in their lives.

Every time you communicate your love to your children and grandchildren, you are building your legacy of love. It should be expressed in spoken words, but you may have to start by writing the words if you aren't used to saying them.

In fact, I'd say every child ought to have the words "I love you" in his or her dad's and grandpa's handwriting. You might consider inscribing a bracelet for your daughter and granddaughter like this:

I love you.

—Dad/Grandpa

On the National Center for Fathering website (fathers .com) we constantly update suggestions for how to show your kids and grandkids you love them. Put these things into practice and you will expand a legacy of love in your family.

Loving God

I mentioned earlier that how we love is based on our experience of God's love for us. Let's come full circle and think about our love for God. Here's my opening question: Do your kids and grandkids know you love God? How?

If you and I have a hard time saying "I love you" to our wives, kids, and grandkids, at least we're being consistent when we hesitate to say "I love you" to God. But that's not a pattern that builds the kind of legacy we want.

If we've discovered that God really loves us, we will want to say "I love you" back to Him. At this point, it's the "why" and the "how" that trips us up.

One thing men usually think is, *Why does God need my love? After all, He's God.* And we're right—God doesn't *need* anything from us. He's not insecure or lonely and in need of a hug.

But here's the thing we miss: Because God really loves us, everything He asks of us—even loving Him—is ultimately for our good!

When we express our love to God, we benefit from a proper view of ourselves as creatures and of God as the creator. We grow by developing affection and intimacy with God. When we love God, we're becoming more like the humans He originally designed us to be.

Likewise, our kids learn the proper biblical worldview when we teach them to say "thank you." When the grandkids are over and Grandma fixes her special muffins, I want to set the pace for them by saying, "Thank you for the muffins, Grandma!" And we do this because it's good and right to affirm another person's gift to us.

But there's a deeper reason we whisper, "Say 'thank you'" in our children's ear as soon as they can talk. We want to help them learn to be grateful. We want them to know others don't have to be kind to them. Otherwise, they are in danger of thinking, *People do so many nice things for me; I must be pretty great!* If we never learn to be grateful, we are likely to think we deserve to be treated a certain way.

The command to love God has similar benefits for us. He pours good things into our lives that express His love, and loving Him back helps us remember that we don't deserve or earn any of His expressions of love for us.

Loving God helps us grow in love for others, which is why there are two parts to the Great Commandment: Love God with all we've got, and love our neighbor as ourselves.

That's some of the *why* of loving God.

Now let's think about the *how*.

Mark 12:30 says to love God "with all your heart and with all your soul and with all your mind and with all your strength." As I said, pretty much all we've got.

Loving with our hearts is actually the easiest part of this commandment. But if we're not comfortable with our emotions, it's the hardest to start doing. This is because, as men, the circle of people we feel loving toward can be small.

If you ask most men, "So, do you feel like you love God?" they will probably give you that "deer in the headlights" look. It takes a while for us to figure out how we feel about God. So let's set that one aside for the moment.

With all your soul

Loving God with all your soul isn't about feelings; it's about your very core connecting with the God who made you, and realizing you want that connection no matter what.

As men, we want to be consistent; feelings are uncomfortable because they are completely inconsistent. You can't count on a feeling to last more than a few moments. And the best feelings seem to vanish almost as soon as we notice them.

So when it comes to the most important things in life, we want to base our actions on something deeper and more consistent and dependable than feelings. That deeper, central place in you and me is the soul. This is why Jesus warned, "What good is it for a man to gain the whole world, yet forfeit his soul?" (Mark 8:36).

If we don't understand this question, it doesn't matter what else we know. Trust settles in the soul. It doesn't get deeper than that. When you've engaged this central part of yourself, you realize that opening yourself to God allows you to say the words to that old song, "It is well with my soul."

You can model loving God with all your soul for your grandkids by deliberately telling them at odd, common, or unusual times how much you appreciate that God knows and loves you—and them. Don't wait for a religious setting.

Ask God to give you teachable moments when you can say, while looking into your grandchild's eyes, "Let me stop everything right now and tell you that I love God, and I love Grandma—and I love you." They need to know they are loved by you in the same way that you love the most important people in your life.

With all your mind

Loving God with all of our minds involves learning to think clearly about God. That happens as we let God speak into our lives through His Word (the Bible) and by His Spirit. If you've settled things in your soul with God, your mind will find it easier to consider who God is and what He expects. If you try to start with the mind and think your way to God while your soul hides in the bushes, your mind will always be unsettled.

If you insist on having every question answered and every doubt dissolved before you trust God, you'll never trust Him. You're not giving room for faith. The Bible describes a process in which we *first* present ourselves to God as living sacrifices, and *then* our minds are renewed:

> Therefore, I urge you, brothers, in view of God's mercy, to offer your bodies as living sacrifices, holy and pleasing to God—this is your spiritual act of worship. Do not conform any longer to the pattern of this world, but be transformed by the renewing of your mind. Then you will be able to test and approve what God's will is—his good, pleasing and perfect will.
>
> ROMANS 12:1-2

The picture of offering your body as a living sacrifice to God should strike a deep chord in your soul—you were created for this kind of surrender to God. That surrender is followed by the "renewing of your mind"—training yourself to think by God's pattern rather than your own, and that is a lifetime pursuit.

Engage your grandkids in thinking about God. When they are young, ask them to draw pictures of what they think God is like. Affirm their efforts, gently correct mistakes, and tell them all the ways God's Word and God's Son have taught you about God. Brainstorm with them ways in which we can show love to God. Help them understand that one of the best ways we show God how much we love Him is by the way we love one another and people who need love.

With all your strength

Loving God with all of your strength is "guy" territory. We want to do something active for God out of love for Him. But our love for God demonstrated in strength is a little like my grandson helping me push the lawnmower. He's giving it all he has, but if I'm not moving the machine, it's not going anywhere.

When it comes to doing things for God, I can never forget I'm still a child working alongside Him, and He's doing most of the work. But the fact that you and I would want to work for God is itself evidence that God is working in us! Philippians 2:13 says, "For it is God who works in you to will and to act according to his good purpose."

With all your heart

Now we're ready for loving God with our whole heart. Now that I'm a grandfather, I'm not as afraid of my feelings as I was when I was a young athlete with a certain reputation I felt I needed to maintain. Shedding tears, especially in public, wasn't part of my profile.

Many men live their entire lives believing the line Tom Hanks' character says in *A League of Their Own*: "There's no crying in baseball!" Except that they apply the statement to all of life, thinking that "crying" represents feelings, and concluding that life should be without feelings.

I know better now. Feelings are emotional responses, and we must do something with them.

Take tears: They can mean many things. I have a friend who jokes that one of the questions he wants to ask God is why tears aren't at least color coded so we would have some idea of what they mean.

Tears can spring from anger, love, sadness, frustration, joy, fear, pain, etc. If you're like me, you're never quite sure why your wife is crying (but it's a safe bet to assume you're responsible!). And here's the amazing thing—sometimes our wives cry because we did something right!

When it comes to loving God with our hearts, we must learn to recognize our feelings. We have them, and they should be part of the way we relate to God each day. There may be some tears in your future as you love God, and you may also have to figure out what they mean. Tears could be a very good thing!

When David asked himself, "Why are you downcast, O my soul? Why so disturbed within me? Put your hope in God, for I will yet praise him, my Savior and my God" (Psalm 43:5), he was identifying feelings, but he was also reminding himself that God was bigger than what he was feeling in the moment. He was loving God with his heart, even when he was feeling down.

Love the Lord your God with all your heart, all your soul, all your mind, and all your strength. There will be a huge, empty canyon in your legacy of love if it doesn't include your personal relationship with God. Believe it or not, the way you love God is the biggest factor in the way you love others.

God designed us to love from top to bottom, with no exceptions:

We love because he first loved us. If anyone says, "I love God," yet hates his brother, he is a liar. For anyone who does not love his brother, whom he has seen, cannot love God, whom he has not seen. And he has given us this command: Whoever loves God must also love his brother.

I JOHN 4:19-21

Last Thought

Why did I spend so much time in this chapter on loving God? Because it's at the center of what matters in life. Let's go back to what Jesus said in Mark 8:36: "What good is it for a man to gain the whole world, yet forfeit his soul?" Developing a legacy of love is about gaining what's most important—a world of love—and keeping your soul.

Wouldn't you want your family to summarize your life this way?

"Grandpa loved Grandma, he loved us, and he really loved God. He showed us what a person is like when he knows down deep that God loves him."

Now that's a legacy of love.

Action Steps

1. Have you sensed any glaring matters needing attention in your life? If I love my children and grandchildren, I'm willing to correct and instruct them as well as affirm and encourage them. Because He loves us, we can expect God to show us things in ourselves that need to change. Do you see any

gaping holes in your legacy of love? What can you do about them?

2. In the lyrics of an old pop song, the songwriter says how difficult it is to express his love at the right time and in the right way. Finally he decides to say "I love you" in a song. Maybe words aren't your thing. Complete this phrase in as many ways as you can to understand how you show love:

When I really love someone, I show it by:

_____.

3. There are many ways to show love, and different people have different ways of communicating love. One of the best books on this type of communication is *The Five Love Languages* by Gary Chapman. Gary suggests that there are five basic ways we love and that each of us tends to favor one of those ways. While we are able to speak a little of each love language, we tend to express love in one way more than others—by offering words of affirmation, acts of service, quality time, gifts, or meaningful touch.[1] Most, if not all, the people in your life may have a love language different from yours. While you may be sure you're expressing pure love to them, they may not actually feel loved. They may actually feel more love from you when you "accidentally speak their language" than when you intentionally try to love them in your customary way.

CHAPTER EIGHT

A LEGACY OF COACHING

No BRAGGING INTENDED, but I've been privileged to count among my friends and acquaintances some of the greatest living and legendary coaches of my lifetime. I've had the opportunity to hang out with Tom Landry, Tony Dungy, Tom Osborne—and those are just the "T names" that come to mind immediately.

I met many of these amazing men when I served on the staff of the Fellowship of Christian Athletes. Their credentials and reputations earned them a place at the table, while I was only in the room because of the organization I represented. What we did share were important ministry goals.

Later on, friendships developed as life kept bringing us together. Their influence in my life went far beyond a shared passion for sports, and I will forever be grateful for each of them and for what I learned from them.

These men and many others I could mention have left a legacy of coaching. Their personalities, combined with their philosophies and work ethic, left a mark on their particular sports.

I realize the influence of these men on my life when I find myself using sports metaphors and concepts to make points about other aspects of life. That's one reason I find the fundamental of coaching so powerful; another is that I was coached—on and off the field—by some great men. Great coaches develop an understanding of their players and their sport that often applies to situations far from the field and for a long time after the game is over.

This principle of coaching takes on special weight for grandfathering. Now that I'm in my sixties, it's amazing to think about the knowledge and life skills influential men were transferring to me and the other players all those years ago.

I think about the times when a coach pulled me to the sideline, looked me in the eye, and spoke from the heart. He knew I could do better, and in the heat of competition he wanted to send a clear message.

I'm not sure I always listened as well as I should have. But looking back, I realize these coaches gave me golden opportunities to benefit and improve, whether or not I took advantage of them. They faithfully did their part.

That's what coaches do! Usually their best physical years are behind them, so they're trying to transfer what they know so their players can succeed. They're dispensing years of experience and wisdom to the next generation.

Successful coaches have had a chance to reflect on a huge assortment of game situations and can see the patterns that consistently lead to good outcomes. Since they are not competing with their players, they are also able to observe and analyze their players' skills and point out areas for improvement, encourage areas of progress, and utilize those athletes in the best possible ways.

Sometimes grandfather-coaching is actually *coaching*. Maybe one or more of your grandkids enjoys an activity that you are completely inept in or that isn't interesting to you at all! Herein is love; not that you already have knowledge and fascination with their interests, but that you are willing to learn enough to *become* interested.

When his granddaughter suddenly expressed an interest in volleyball, one grandfather spent time watching games and reading articles so he would better understand the sport. When they discussed her performance, he not only encouraged her, he was able to use the right terminology to describe what he saw her doing well. The coaching went beyond the volleyball court.

More and more I realize that the focus of my coaching needs to be on my grandchildren. I'm not replacing their parents or competing for their primary coaching roles in their children's lives; I'm more like the assistant coach who has some special duties, and on particular occasions I can speak to individual players on the team with the weight and wisdom of experience.

Here's how this works in practice. Make the question "How can I help?" a common statement when visiting your adult children. Let them assign you duties. Let the kids know that you see yourself as Assistant Coach Grandpa, reporting for duty. And be ready for anything.

I'm assuming you changed your children's diapers—now it's time to dust off that old skill. But realize that your memory of diapers may be significantly different from the new-fangled things babies are wearing now. You may have to have one of your kids school you up on the basics.

If you're in their home, make sure you help the grandkids keep their parents' rules. As the grandkids grow older, ask their parents how you can best back up what they are teaching their children. Let the parents know you are committed to helping them.

So when it comes to coaching your grandkids, get used to the idea that you're an assistant, not the head coach anymore. You may be the patriarch of the family, particularly when your own father dies, but your role will be much less "hands on" than it was in the past. You may be relegated to the role of babysitter, but relish it!

There may also come a time when you're privileged to receive a specific coaching assignment from your child when he or she says, "Dad, you've always been good at _____. Can you give your grandson/granddaughter some pointers?"

Your child is trusting you with what is most precious to him or her. Guard that trust, Grandpa.

Practicing Humility

At this point, I need to always remind myself of what I say to fathers: Dad, even though you are wise, there's another factor that comes into play. *You have to be humble* to coach your children. You have to be sensitive and listen to what they're saying *first*, and that takes humility.

I realize that the pace of life today presents some special challenges to listening well, and as men, we sometimes get the feeling that what's happening is all about us. It's easy to think, "I'm the patriarch of the family. I know what's best, and here's what we need to do."

Now I see how this philosophy works when a child might be doing something dangerous and she needs to obey before we can sit down and talk about the situation. Running into the street or poking metal objects into electrical outlets might lead to "What were you thinking?" but instant obedience to the command "Stop!" must happen first.

But we are not in a good place if most of our interactions with our grandkids display an attitude that says, "I haven't got time to listen to you or explain my reasons for what I'm telling you—you just have to obey." They may hear that from their parents, but we should be moving at a different pace. Deliberately.

When we take time to listen and to explain, we actually increase the likelihood that they will obey instantly when that's required. We're assistant coaches, so we can take a few moments to talk with the grandkids about why Mom and Dad sometimes issue orders that require instant obedience. We can tell them that their parents may sound angry or scared sometimes because they love their children and want to keep them around to give them grandchildren—like we have!

Grandpa, part of our advantage is that we should have time to listen. We shouldn't be in a hurry. You may become a grandfather at the height of your working years, but you should also take your new position in life as a strong hint to put things in order so you can start relating to the next generation.

Fortunately, your grandchildren will be babies for a little while, so you have some time to get serious about the situation, but don't procrastinate.

Solomon made some astute comments about time. The well-known verses begin, "There is a time for everything, and a season for every activity under heaven: a time to be born and a time to die, a time to plant and a time to uproot, a time to kill and a time to heal, a time to tear down and a time to build" (Ecclesiastes 3:1-3).

Solomon's point is there are certain designated times in life for certain purposes, and if we miss them, we miss an opportunity. There's a time to be involved in your grandchildren's lives, and if you put it off or treat it casually and it passes, you won't get it back. If this is your time to be Grandpa, don't miss it!

Along with listening, coaching in a family setting requires humility. You are practicing this valuable trait when you say, "I want what's best for you, whether you listen to me or not. Because it's not about me." It's less about who gets recognized, and more about fulfilling a responsibility to the next generation.

That's what I'm realizing more and more—the *responsibility* I have to my family. It affects how I talk to them, how I touch them, and how I hold them—how intentional I am when I'm with them.

I'm discovering humility when I remember that I'm not

the first level of authority in my grandchildren's lives. It's very easy to unintentionally step on young parents' toes.

Comments that we think are helpful observations or even just common sense advice can cause our children to feel as if we're not letting them be adults and the parents of their children.

It's one thing to answer our children frankly if they ask us a question; it's another to offer unsolicited parenting advice. We may want to jump into coaching mode with our married kids, but we'd better take a step back and be willing to wait for permission.

With the level of confusion and dysfunction in families today, we're hearing more about grandparents' rights. Making demands about access to the grandkids, however, usually doesn't allow for healthy interaction with their parents or the grandchildren. One way to make sure we see our grandkids even less is to complain.

Humility is also required knowing that I'm probably not the only grandfather in my grandchildren's lives. One of us probably sees the grandkids more often than the other.

We need to keep the absent grandfather in the picture as much as possible. A good working relationship with him will bring benefits to your kids' marriage and to the grandchildren.

I know one couple who made a significant effort to visit and get to know the parents of each of their four children-in-law. They did this even though those other parents were living in three different states and another country.

This brings me to the special role of your children's marriage partners. By the time your kids get married, your relationship with them is already shaped from years of loving, coaching, and modeling—which you've done in a certain way. But how you relate to your kids will most likely be different from how your children-in-law relate to their parents.

I have two sons-in-law and a daughter-in-law, and each of them is a treasure to me, a part of my family. But I have to remind myself that someone else raised them. That means I can't assume they received the same type of coaching my kids did, even if it was good. This is another great reason to get to know the family of your in-laws. You may be in for some great coaching from them!

While it's true that we can pass on helpful knowledge and wisdom through coaching, be cautious about offering coaching to your children once they have spouses. Your married children are part of your family, but they are also building something new. They will need space, and may well misread your good intentions as meddling.

Believe me—it's hard to get this right. An uninvited suggestion about car maintenance, house organization, lawn care, or anything else can sound as if we're saying, "You're doing it wrong!"

There are countless matters about family life where the choices others make will be different from ours, but it doesn't mean they are wrong.

I've talked with many grandparents who had to step back and apologize for unintentional offenses—it's all part of figuring out the balance between offering and providing help when it's wanted and living with the truth that sometimes it's not needed or wanted! Even though we want to be needed and wanted.

I can remember when each of my kids brought home potential mates I wasn't thrilled with. Sometimes we were asked to give our opinion, but often we were not. I had to largely hold my peace and let the training my bride and I had instilled in our kids do its work. I'm glad I did, and I'm delighted with the choices my kids eventually made.

Our kids have sometimes said, "Yeah, Pop, we knew those weren't the right ones for us, but we're glad you let us have some space to figure it out!" I'm still trying to walk that same fine line now that I'm relating to all these grandkids!

Granddad, I hope you're learning to give your kids and grandkids space to learn. Encourage and advise; resist controlling. Ultimately, you and I have to develop the humility to know that our grandkids (like our children) are placed in our lives for safekeeping, not ownership. God has temporarily entrusted them to us.

We need to remember that we're transferring our accumulated wisdom. We can't predict or determine how or even if it's going to be used. We give it away, just as it was given to us. And we're leading our children toward character and their own personal responsibilities.

That's what coaches do.

Coaching with Stories

Not long ago, Focus on the Family invited me to compile a number of brief articles on the subject of fathering from some of the greatest leaders today. We called the book *The 21-Day Dad's Challenge: Three Weeks to a Better Relationship with Your Kids.* When I asked my son Marcellus if he'd like to contribute a chapter, it didn't occur to me that he would write observations about me!

The topic he chose was the importance of a dad as a storyteller. He highlighted different phases of his childhood—when we lived in Chicago and then Kansas City—referring to the way stories were part of life in those places.

I was like my dad in that we both used the captive audience during a car drive to do some coaching; my father did this by sharing wise little lessons, and I did it by telling stories.

Marcellus pointed out that I came alive as a storyteller when we would visit my childhood places and I'd tell stories about his grandparents and the world we lived in. Seen through my son's eyes, my father and others from his generation lived an amazing story, and I was the storyteller.

Now Marcellus has a deep appreciation for his heritage. He realizes much of the opportunity to develop a good life for his family and himself was secured for him by choices his grandparents made when this country was largely still segregated and career choices for African Americans were limited.

He's trying to blend his father's love for storytelling with his grandfather's love for wisdom—so more power to him!

Here's what you may discover, Grandpa. As your children and grandchildren express an interest in the family past, their questions and curiosity will spur you to remember. My son's questions have made me recall things about his grandfather that I never realized while I was growing up.

I've been able to look back and appreciate what it took for Pop to begin work at a VA hospital at an entry-level position but gradually work his way into a significant place in that institution. He trained and advised many of the staff who actually held higher positions because they realized his longevity, experience, and wisdom gave him a unique perspective. He was willing to share that accumulated knowledge with others.

Toward the end of his life, he was a patient in that hospital, wearing his patient identification alongside his credentials as an official volunteer and still dispensing his unique insights to others. It wasn't unusual to find young doctors sitting by his bed, consulting with Mr. Casey about the challenges of their jobs.

Helping my kids and grandkids to be proud of their grandfather or great-grandfather reminds me how proud I am to be his son.

Not everyone is a storyteller. But everyone has stories. You are a story. So find a way to tell it. Be ready to answer your grandkids' questions, and you will find yourself telling them things that sound like stories even if you're not known for spinning a yarn. If you let them, they'll drag the adventures out of you.

Maybe you're not proud of your heritage. Perhaps there's shame you have to overcome or a pattern you have to break. Whatever you have to face about your family, remember this: They produced you.

Don't try to make them something they were not, but remember that they gave you the gift of life and something that drives you to make it a good one. So find a way to be grateful that people who may have done so many things wrong got something right. Use your story to coach your grandkids about a good way to live.

Be a Team Player

As the grandkids grow older, find out what your kids are trying to teach them and back up their efforts. Those grandkids need to know their parents and grandparents are a tag team that can wear them out if necessary!

So if one of your kids drops off the grandkids and mentions, "We're trying to teach him to say 'Thank you'" or "We've noticed she needs to share more with her little brother," you will need to put that on your mental radar to include in the conversation as you observe their interactions.

I remember my grandparents often telling me the same things my parents did, but somehow it sounded weightier in their deep or gravelly voices. Sometimes grandparents just have a different way of illustrating or explaining something that makes sense to a child. In any case, young people benefit from hearing the same truths from as many different sources as possible.

When the grandkids are young, being a team player is often a matter of outlasting the kids physically. When my bride and I take on the grandkids at this stage of their lives, a day together wipes us out.

We love getting tired this way. It reminds us how much energy it takes to parent little kids. Like most grandparents remembering our own child-rearing years, we look at each other occasionally and ask, "How did we do it, babe?"

The real answer to that question is, "We probably didn't do it alone, did we?" Maybe we had parents living close by who pitched in, or a great relationship with friends from church, or a neighbor who helped in different ways.

If you pulled off the parenting thing without any help,

then you might be the best qualified to know how much help parents need. Your experiences are golden motivations to come alongside the next generation and lend a hand or whisper encouragement.

Life Drills

The role of grandparents can be crucial in the way faith is transmitted from one generation to another. Often, parents set a pattern for faith (or lack of it) in the home, but it's the grandparents who interpret the pattern for the grandchildren.

"Why do we go to church on Sunday, Grandpa?" is a question you should be ready to answer in a way they can understand.

Grandkids may well see inconsistencies between their nuclear-family lifestyle and yours, but realize that their first questions probably stem more from curiosity than anything else.

So if the question above becomes "How come you and Grandma go to church every Sunday, but we don't go very often?" that's not an opportunity to take a shot at the kids' poor church attendance.

Focus on why you do what you do rather than interpreting their parents' behavior for them, particularly if the comparison would sound negative. Before you answer a grandchild's question, it's worth taking a moment to ask yourself, "What will this sound like back home if this child says, 'Grandpa said _____'?"

In other words, don't say things to or do things with your grandchildren that you wouldn't say or do with your own children present.

I sincerely hope that you and I would never want to intentionally or unintentionally create additional problems in our families. But I also know that we live in a seriously messed-up world. You may get a call from an upset grown child or in-law that starts out, "Did you really tell our son/daughter that _____!?"

In that moment you will realize that some grandkids are reporters who will give a moment-by-moment account of everything that happened at Grandma and Grandpa's house. Like a reporter, sometimes they'll get it right and sometimes they'll get it wrong. So let me offer a little coaching on how you respond.

First, thank them for calling you directly, acknowledge their concern, and affirm their right to be concerned if you said something like what was reported to them. Rather than defend the specifics, state again that your intention is always to back them up. Emphasize to the best of your ability that you are always trying to encourage and help them and their kids, not undercut them.

Then, if what you said was reported accurately and you now realize it came across in a way that undermined or questioned the parents, it's time to apologize. Offer to apologize to the child also.

If what you said was reported inaccurately, don't throw the grandchild under the bus by accusing them of lying, but calmly state what you did say and recognize how it might have been heard in the wrong way. State again that you value the opportunity to support what they are doing as parents, and thank them for the chance to clarify and make things right.

Keep the big picture in mind: Your ongoing relationship

with your children and grandchildren is more precious than an instance when you said the wrong thing or were misunderstood.

When in doubt about things that might come up in conversations with your grandkids, it's wise to alert their parents when you hand them back.

Telling your kids, "By the way, she asked about _____, and we told her _____" or "The subject of _____ came up and we said _____ and then encouraged him to ask you about it" keeps the communication open between the generations.

As an assistant coach, you are giving the head coach a heads-up on how practice went. You are also continuing to build a legacy of coaching, making use of opportunities to speak into the lives of the next generation.

One Basic

In my mind, one of the most important things every child needs to learn is how to pray. How your kids and grandkids relate to their heavenly Father will touch every other decision they make in life. This might be even more of a focus for me now that I'm a granddad.

I mentioned earlier about how I do my morning prayers in our "Carolina room." It's comforting when I see that my grandkids know what I do in there. I'm praying they become people of prayer, even as I'm still learning to be a man of prayer as a granddad.

The other day, we had a bunch of our grandkids at the house, and I took it a step further. While we were all in the Carolina room, I sat down at the prayer spot and walked them through some of what I do there. This was a sweet spot of grandfather coaching for me.

I pulled out each of their photos and told them, "I pray every day for God's blessings for each one of you. And I pray for your mom and dad and their marriage and what they do every day."

I showed them a photo of their grandma, my bride, and talked about how I pray for her every day too. It was just a casual conversation, but it got me thinking: *How do our children and grandchildren learn how to pray?*

They learn much about prayer by listening to others pray.

I remember the story of one young family with three children and the experience they had praying together when the kids went to bed at night. The two boys in the family were old enough to participate in the prayer time themselves while their little sister sat or lay in her crib listening. After the boys prayed, Mom and Dad would pray.

One night, when that little girl was about two, Dad heard something soft as he was finishing his prayer. He looked over to find his daughter with her hands folded in prayer just like her bigger brothers.

Even though she still couldn't speak, she was mumbling as if she were praying like the rest of the family. She was imitating even before she understood what it was all about.

Coaching in these important lessons can begin at a young age. And Granddad, that process absolutely needs to include you! Example is a great teacher.

I also encourage you to *talk* with your grandkids about prayer—how it works—and even about prayer strategies. Be sure to include stories about times when you prayed and how

God answered. Let them know that the biggest thing God does when we pray is change us. Start by just reaffirming that prayer is a conversation with our heavenly Father, who wants only the best for us.

Children love to hear their name in prayer (and so do we). Let them hear you pray for them—specifically. Make the prayers about their immediate needs. Your care for them communicates God's care for them.

Help them think about different places they can pray, different postures, and what things are worth praying for. What does it mean to pray "in Jesus' name"? Is it really possible to "pray without ceasing" as it says in the Bible? Can the way you live be a prayer? Ask them, "Is prayer more for God or more for us?" What about that mysterious word, "Amen"?

That reminds me of a story a friend told me about trying to teach prayer to a large number of children at a vacation Bible school. The group had an interesting discussion about the meaning of *amen*.

One kid said, "I don't think it means anything; it's just that sound you make at the end of the prayer so everyone knows you're done." My friend had to agree with his observation; that's just how many of us use the term.

Then he told them that the word is borrowed from another language (Hebrew) and it means "so be it" or "truly." In a moment of inspiration he said, "It's like ending your prayer but stopping for a moment to say, 'And I mean it!'" *Amen* emphasizes what we just said. It tells God that we weren't just saying some words; we were doing our best to let Him know what is important to us and trusting Him to do what's best.

The kids immediately started putting that into practice,

not only in that class but also throughout the church. A number of people were surprised in the weeks to come when they prayed in public and their closing "Amen" was immediately followed by a chorus of young voices saying, "And I mean it!"

Whatever their ages, impress the vital importance of prayer on your grandchildren. Show them how to pray, and pray with them.

Kids will tend to learn one prayer to begin with, and if they are not encouraged to explore other phrases and names for God, they may simply repeat the first prayer they ever learned.

Coach your grandkids by reminding them how you enjoy all the different conversations you have with them. It might be a little boring if every time you were with them they said the same thing over and over.

Coachable Moments

You can't plan most coachable moments. You can't predict what will present you with an opportunity to school grandchildren on something important.

You might see something on the street or be confronted with an unexpected scene on TV that causes your grandkids to ask questions or look to see your reaction. They might bring up something they heard or saw and wonder what you think. Don't let those moments pass.

Make it a point to highlight good things you see, and try to talk about people who are doing admirable things. It's easy for us to look at the broken world with a negative outlook that ends up complaining about everything.

Our grandkids also need to hear us tell them what's right in the world, about the places where they can invest their efforts when they grow up. They need to know that we do more than worry about the world.

Remember what Paul told the Philippians to think about instead of wasting time worrying? "Finally, brothers, whatever is true, whatever is noble, whatever is right, whatever is pure, whatever is lovely, whatever is admirable—if anything is excellent or praiseworthy—think about such things" (Philippians 4:8).

We can notice such things and point them out to our grandkids.

But that doesn't mean you shouldn't have a list of things you'd like to teach your grandkids someday. This is like a bucket list—things you want to do and places you want to go while you're alive. Except this list represents what you want to pass on to your grandkids' generation.

What skills have you learned along the way, either when you were a kid yourself or as you grew up? Keep a list in the notebook with your family tree. Check off and date when you talk about those things, even though multiple grandkids and various occasions may mean repeated conversations.

We can pass on all sorts of basic skills someone taught us or that we learned by trial and error. Tying shoes, knotting a tie, or changing a tire are just a few examples. Cooking, woodworking, auto maintenance, writing, carrying on conversations—all these involve basic skills that don't necessarily come naturally.

Certain social skills can be taught by Grandpa: holding a door for someone, especially a lady; greeting people on the street; showing concern for a friend; expressing appreciation to a military man or woman for his or her sacrifice. If the grandkids don't notice, ask them if they understand why you did that: "Do you know why I thanked that man in uniform for his service?"

One set of grandparents I know included their grandchildren in a Jesus' birthday party during the Christmas season. This was Grandma's brainchild, but Grandpa was pulled in big time. Each year was a different theme.

One year they bought five miniature Christmas trees, which each of the grandchildren decorated. Then they took the trees to a nearby nursing home. The grandkids visited rooms where there were few or no decorations, asking the residents if they would mind adopting a tree for the season.

The residents were delighted with the visit and the decorations. Much to the grandparents' surprise, the grandkids themselves began to sing Christmas carols as they visited the residents, which led not only to delivering the trees but also to mini-concerts in each room!

Another year, the grandkids handmade Christmas cards and delivered them to the rooms of veterans in a different nursing home, taking a moment during the season to thank those vets for their service.

It took some planning and coaching on the part of the grandparents, but the grandkids had a great time. Those kids can now look back on their childhood with memories of a legacy of coaching provided by their grandparents.

Action Steps

If you're already coaching the grandkids, way to go, Grandpa! These ideas are intended to help you be the best assistant coach you can be.

1. Look at your list of grandkids and each of their interests in your heritage/legacy notebook. How many of those interests are present in situations in which you can function in some way as a coach? It's good to run any new plan by the grandchild's parents to make sure they agree.

2. Are you involved in continuing education because you are keeping up with your grandkids' interests? What are some opportunities to expand your own horizons?

3. Do you know where the boundaries are in your role as a grandparent? If you don't, consider having that important conversation with your child and child-in-law.

CHAPTER NINE

A LEGACY OF MODELING

As a young father, you probably learned that your kids watched everything you did and listened to everything you said. Your grandkids do the same: They remember what we think they didn't even hear.

A set of grandparents had quite a jolt one Sunday while leaving for church with their three-year-old granddaughter. Grandma and Grandpa found themselves a little behind schedule that morning because this little person was added to the mix.

After the three of them hurried to the car and buckled in, Grandpa began backing the car out of the driveway. That's when the granddaughter practically shouted from the back seat, "Grandma! Where's your Bible?"

That little girl had learned at home that we don't leave for church without our Bibles in hand. Grandpa ran back inside to retrieve his bride's Bible, chuckling with delight every moment.

You can't be sure what your grandkids will pick up along the way, but you can try to make sure they don't learn the *wrong* things from you.

There I was, helping my daughter fasten her kids into their car seats when my four-year-old grandson responded by uttering a one-word exclamation that stopped us in our tracks. It was not an R-rated word, or even PG-13, but was definitely one his parents do not want him to use. My daughter stopped, looked at him very seriously, and said, "Where did you learn that?"

It's a classic parenting situation, right?

My grandson grinned broadly, looked right at me, and said, "From Pi-Pa." In case you don't remember, that's what my grandkids call me! I am Pi-Pa. And my grandson had just thrown me under the bus! He was falsely accusing me of teaching him this forbidden word!

Further questioning by his mother (while I sat in the hot seat) revealed that he couldn't remember where he had heard the word, but it hadn't been from Pi-Pa. Close call!

This incident wasn't earth-shattering, but it reminded me of the power that fathers and grandfathers have as models of behavior and character. Children imitate our behavior. Sometimes it's cute, as when your toddler pushes his plastic mower behind his dad as he cuts the grass. Other times it's not so cute. How often do we hear a child let loose with some profanity and then say, "I heard it from Daddy"?

Looking in the Mirror

Before we talk about what we *should* model for our grand-kids, let's talk about another side of modeling.

Unlike the *intentional* teaching and coaching we discussed in the last chapter, modeling can be what we do *unintentionally* that leaves a mark on others' lives.

While it's true that we need to demonstrate only the behavior we want from our grandkids, we can take it a step further. I was telling a friend about that incident with my grandson, and he pointed out that while I don't use that word, I do often use another word when I'm surprised or excited about something. It isn't a cuss word, but it's also not that far from the word my grandson repeated. Ouch!

With modeling, we need to avoid doing or saying things we don't want our children doing or saying—as well as things they might *confuse* with the wrong behavior. We don't want to cause these kids to stumble or sin—the Bible cautions against that in numerous places.

It has been rightly said that more is "caught" than "taught" when it comes to the way we influence our children and grandchildren. They are watching us as much or more than they are hearing us, so we should be conscious about what they see.

Because we seldom know how other people (and the grand-kids) see us, we need reminders to be humble. Fortunately, God has given us some help.

Even the best "mirror" would fail to give us an accurate reading of our true selves and our impact on others. Jesus' half-brother James knew this well:

Do not merely listen to the word, and so deceive yourselves. Do what it says. Anyone who listens to the word but does not do what it says is like a man who looks at his face in a mirror and, after looking at himself, goes away and immediately forgets what he looks like. But the man who looks intently into the perfect law that gives freedom, and continues to do this, not forgetting what he has heard, but doing it—he will be blessed in what he does.

JAMES 1:22-25

He's right. Only the "perfect law that gives freedom" can give us an accurate reading of ourselves when we take the time to read it. James is talking about the Bible, the source God has provided to give us reliable direction about how to live our lives in such a way that we will be blessed.

And there can be no greater blessing than to leave behind a model of godly living for others to follow. That's what a legacy of modeling can create for your descendants.

Now none of us can be perfect role models, and thank goodness we can always ask for forgiveness and even use our own mistakes as proof that we all need God's grace.

But gentlemen, will you join me in our humble quest to be models of excellence?

Modeling and Work

Because work consumes so much of a man's time, we instantly connect our work with being a role model. But it's not easy to know the difference between modeling hard work and providing an example of a workaholic.

My family is a huge part of my life; investing in my bride, my children, and grandchildren is a top priority, no question. At the same time, I love my job! The message I hear from society is that work is the primary place to create a legacy, and my job gives me a sense of purpose.

This can cause tension. That purpose isn't easy to turn off when I get home. There are always more good things I could do to make a difference, and they seem to have a sense of urgency.

Not long ago I came face-to-face with this dilemma. My daughter, who doesn't live nearby, was visiting our home with her children, and it was a busy time for me at the office. At home, there were all kinds of shenanigans going on with the grandkids. They were running around the house, playing games, eating meals—doing all that great stuff I like to enjoy as a granddad.

One morning during her visit I was about to walk out the door to work, but I stopped. None of the grandkids were up yet, and I realized I couldn't wait all day to see them! I had to call my office and delay my arrival a few minutes so I could say good morning to those kids.

Then one evening it all became clear. People were calling and texting me about different work matters, and I looked over into the next room and saw the rest of the family "doing life" without me.

I was convicted! Those grandchildren needed my attention. I thought of them as lumps of clay, being molded into adults. They have great parents, but I also have a role to play.

So that evening, I silenced my phone and put it in the other room. I gave my staff and myself the evening off for the purpose of family health. I decided that those moments at home are more important than the work demands, which never go away.

I also realized that my work with the National Center for Fathering wouldn't mean much if my own family didn't experience the benefits of our research on the impact of dads and granddads. How could I keep talking the talk of responsible fathering if I wasn't walking that walk on my own turf?

Granddad, I don't know what your situation might be. I suppose all of our work situations are different in some ways, so I can't make suggestions that will be effective for everyone. But I urge you to really consider how "present" you are when you're home from your job. We all need to provide for our families, but I hope you're not missing those priceless family times that can happen any evening or morning.

And don't try to do this just when the kids or grandkids are over; make it your lifestyle. Your bride deserves your attention when it's just the two of you. Grandkids can tell the difference between us "putting on a show" and welcoming them into life the way we live it.

Be sensitive to what is claiming your time and attention, and choose to give your best to your family.

Modeling Traditions

I hope there are annual family events on your calendar because they can add significant memories to your legacy project. Whether the event is a holiday or some other get-together, creating traditions provides a way for you to add to your legacy and model the love of our heavenly Father.

Let me give you an example that has developed in our home over many years.

Each Thanksgiving there's plenty of humor around the dinner table as everyone gangs up on Dad, saying, "All right, Dad's gonna ask us, 'What are you thankful for?'" Once we get past the joking, everyone has a chance to recall God's blessings from the past year. I want all of us to be able to see how God has delivered good things in our lives.

Later we'll look for colorful leaves outside with the grandkids, or rake the leaves into a big pile and toss the kids in, one by one.

Eventually, we'll gather our group of ten or twelve for a family photo. If everyone is able to make it, there are eighteen smiling faces! Actually, with all the grandkids, that photo can be quite an adventure. You can be sure it will be added to the treasured visual record of our family.

Most importantly, it's a tradition. And that's my point. Guys, you need to be the quiet power that makes a tradition happen. If you're peeling potatoes or carving the bird, that's great. But I hope you'll also put extra thought into the matter of family traditions.

Why? Because it's a way to deliver a blessing to your family, even when they are not aware of it in the moment. When your kids and grandkids are older, they'll be able to look back and recognize the love you showed them through those traditions.

Keep the old traditions going and add new ones—playing touch football or sharing a family history lesson. Make sure to involve everyone, from the youngest to the oldest. Make it a special goal to bring God back to front and center in your family's lives as you plan an activity.

One of our favorite Christmas traditions involves reading a simple children's book called *The Christmas Story*. It began when my oldest daughter was just a few years old, and now that I'm a granddad, it's something I'm able to share with all the children in the house—old and young.

I realize that in today's world, family situations are complicated. Maybe you can't make it work for everyone to be at your home. Maybe you're a divorced granddad and a hotel room is the only way to be together with your kids and grandkids at Christmas. Or you have family members scattered around, and meeting in a central location is the answer.

In those cases, I'd encourage you to do what you can to keep your family traditions going—wherever you are. For your family, perhaps attending a Christmas Eve service followed by a simple meal may work better than opening gifts on Christmas morning.

The idea is to be flexible in where, when, and how you celebrate now that your kids are married and have another family's traditions to consider. The "every year" may need to shift to "every other year" to honor a variety of family approaches.

If the old traditions are becoming complicated, you can always start new traditions! Don't jump to the conclusion that you don't have any traditions or potential traditions. You might even discover something in your past that can be revived as a reason to gather the family.

One grandfather I know got excited about encouraging his grandson's interest in sailing when he realized that his own father, sister, and daughter were all interested in harnessing the wind, even though he hadn't been on the water much himself.

Do you know of any activities or interests that your grandchild or family members are involved in fairly regularly? A grandchild who takes up a sport or a musical instrument will not only fill up your schedule with games and concerts to attend, he or she may present an opportunity for family gatherings to support that budding athlete or musician.

Some of these events will be a tradition for only a season, but the memory that you were part of your grandchildren's lives will remain with them and may influence how they spend time with their own children and grandchildren.

What events in life might trigger a new tradition? A move might seem to take people apart, but it may also create a greater desire to get together. One set of grandparents with four married children started organizing family reunions once or twice a decade, but as the grandchildren and then great-grandchildren arrived, they began pushing for a gathering every two or three years.

As the family has grown, planning the event has required some creativity. In a recent reunion, twenty-eight extended family members, representing eight individual family units, took over an entire dorm floor at a university campus that was available during the summer and cheaper than a hotel. They also found plenty of free activities to do while they spent time together.

Keep things as simple as possible. Don't call it a tradition until you've done something two or more times. Expect to experiment and not necessarily succeed the first time you try something new with the family. Do your homework too. Try not to step on someone else's plans with your own plans.

Depending on your family, a spontaneous gathering might work better, but don't underestimate the value of planning ahead. A large family outing scheduled a year or more in advance has a better chance of success than one suggested for next month.

Let me tell you about one of my favorite Casey family traditions. It happens on Christmas Eve, when we gather at the fireplace and each open one gift that sets the stage for our time together.

Inevitably, my son Marcellus will look at the present and sarcastically say, "Wow, I wonder what this is!" Because that single Christmas Eve gift is the same every year: flannel pajamas!

We all open our presents and say, "All right: one, two, three—ready, go!" Then everybody runs to a bedroom, puts on the new pajamas, and returns to the living room for a family picture. We now have many years of Christmas Eve pajama pictures in our collection.

I know it might sound silly to some people, but it's what we do. Even as our older three children became teenagers, went to college, and got married, they always looked forward to pajamas on Christmas Eve, and they still do.

So Granddad, if you want to take the "Casey family pajama tradition" and make it your own, go for it! But that's not the point I'm trying to make. Almost anything from a certain meal to a certain event can become the tradition no one wants to miss.

The real point is that traditions are a great tool for creating good memories of shared love. Modeling love through traditions is a goal worth pursuing.

Modeling Commitment

We need always to be mindful about what our children and grandchildren see in our lives.

A woman I know is a youth sponsor at her church. It's an urban church, so she's influencing some kids in tough situations. Recently she had a jaw-dropping experience. She was at a youth group meeting one night when her husband picked her up for their date.

As they were leaving, one of the girls asked, "Where are you guys going?"

"We're going out to celebrate our anniversary," the sponsor answered.

Then the girl asked, "What's an anniversary?"

Think about that a minute. Apparently, this girl had gone through thirteen or fifteen years of life without ever seeing a married couple celebrate their marriage in that way. It could be she'd never seen a couple stay married for any length of time, or maybe being married at all was foreign to her.

Granddad, this should be a reminder for all of us—and for our nation. That girl gave us a picture of where our culture is headed if we don't start reversing our troubling trends. I'm thinking about the thousands, even millions, of kids who don't have a good model of maturity, love, or faithfulness in their lives.

How are you reaching out beyond your family, perhaps to some of your grandkid's friends, to offer an intentional model of healthy adult living?

At the National Center for Fathering, we are working to create a culture known for a high value on marriage, fathers who are committed to their families and involved in their children's lives, and men who love their brides and serve them with love, respect, and commitment. And we want that type of culture to extend to grandfathers, too. When kids see men behaving this way, it gives them security and confidence. It gives them hope.

When I think of anniversaries, I think of the two men who were my main role models in life: my dad, Ralph Casey, and Coach Tom Landry of the Dallas Cowboys. Both were married to their brides for more than fifty years. If the Lord tarries and my health holds up, I fully intend to reach that milestone with Melanie.

That's a legacy I want to pass on to my children and grandchildren. I want them to know what an anniversary is, sure, but more than that, I want them to know what a great marriage is like. I want them to have a profound understanding of faithfulness because they have a living example in front of them.

Not that I'm perfect or anything special, but even imperfect people can find a way to make a marriage work. Maybe that, more than anything else, is the message our culture and the children of tomorrow need to hear. Even more, they need to see it.

Modeling Biblical Happiness

Our society practically screams at us to do whatever it takes to meet our needs and desires. The idea of keeping a promise if it's going to be hard or inconvenient doesn't sound appealing in a world urging us to seek what will make us happy.

Our culture today says, "You deserve to be happy." This is a lie, and the motto of many profoundly unhappy people. It's a consistent aspect of much of the messed-up thinking in our world today:

"I deserve to be happy, so I'm walking away from my marriage."

"I deserve to be happy, so I'm going to try a little unfaithfulness."

"I deserve to be happy, so I'll betray my children by abandoning their mother."

The word *deserve* is misleading. We may deserve many things, but being happy is not one of them. *Deserve* means we have done something to be worthy of or are someone who is simply *owed* a certain experience. This makes "I deserve to be happy" one of the most prideful, self-centered, destructive thoughts a person can have. To rephrase a wise saying, the road to hell is paved with "I deserve to be happy" thoughts.

The framers of our Declaration of Independence said we have the right to *pursue* happiness; we don't have the right to *be* happy.

Yet true happiness is not something we gain by going after it directly; true happiness is a by-product of pursuing the right things: truth, faithfulness, integrity, and the well-being of others. Putting ourselves first cuts us off from happiness; putting others first sets us up for happiness.

As a father and grandfather, you can model for your kids and grandkids the behaviors that lead to happiness, and most of them are not easy. It starts with keeping promises. Don't make promises you can't keep to your grandkids. It's much better to be remembered as a grandfather who was full of surprises you never promised than someone who made promises you never kept.

You can tell your grandchildren that treating others the way they themselves want to be treated won't necessarily mean that they will be treated right, but it will mean that they will have lived the right way—the way their Creator designed them to live. But those words won't mean much unless they see you model those principles.

When a big truck passes you on the highway at night and your grandchild asks, "Grandpa, why did you flash your headlights after he passed you?" you can say, "It's part of courtesy on the road. I'm letting that driver know he can move back over in front of me, because sometimes it's hard for a truck driver to tell."

And when the trucker flashes his running lights, you can say, "And that's a trucker's way of saying, 'Thanks.' Even when we're driving, we want to treat others as we'd like to be treated."

The pattern of all you do (especially what you do when things go wrong) will become your legacy of modeling.

Modeling in Brokenness

My heart goes out to you if you're a single dad and grandfather because of a broken marriage. You have difficult ground to cover just to be with your kids and grandkids. The same is true if one of your kids' marriages fails.

Society may scoff at the idea that divorce causes damage, but denial isn't just a river in Egypt. The devastation is often ignored or denied because it is too deep and too overwhelming. Ignoring or denying doesn't make it any less destructive.

If you find yourself in that place, I'm not eager to find fault or assign blame. But if you don't know why the divorce happened, it might be worth getting some help to figure it out. That way you can make sure it doesn't happen again, and you can warn your children and grandchildren of the danger. You can't rewind the clock or undo what's done, but that doesn't mean you can't do *anything*. And God can certainly do a lot, no matter what!

None of us is a perfect model, but some of us seriously damage others and our relationships through our imperfections. That's why, just as with coaching, an attitude of humility is essential to modeling a godly life. It is humbling to recognize that every relationship includes enough friction and conflict to require forgiveness.

We live in a world the Bible describes as fallen and broken by sin. If we don't forgive and can't ask for forgiveness, our relationships will suffer. And even broken relationships still require forgiveness. You and I can't escape the need to forgive and be forgiven by jumping out of relationships.

If you're tracking with me, you may be wondering just where humility and forgiveness come from. And how do we know we're including these traits in our legacy of modeling?

Humility and forgiveness come from the same place. They originate with God, and they are most clearly modeled in the words and life of His Son, Jesus Christ. There is no greater picture of forgiveness than Jesus—who was mocked, unjustly condemned, beaten, spit on, humiliated, and roughly nailed to a cross—and still said, "Father, forgive them; for they know not what they do" (Luke 23:34, KJV).

Take a moment and replace the "them" in Jesus' statement with your own name. You and I can't get close to the deepest understanding of humility and forgiveness until we see that our sin connects us directly to the reason Jesus had to suffer everything I just mentioned and more. Forgiveness and humility are found at the foot of the Cross.

When the Bible describes humility before God, the word it uses most often is *repentance*. That word means much more than feeling bad or remorseful about what we've done or who we are. It means getting serious enough about what's wrong that we truly want to change. Repentance means confessing our sin, asking God for forgiveness, and expecting His work of cleansing.

We need God's intervention because we can't change ourselves. Plenty of people (you and I are among them) regret bad behavior, but we do it anyway. First John 1:9 tells us what we need to do: "If we confess our sins, he is faithful and just and will forgive us our sins and purify us from all unrighteousness."

Grandpa, if a review of your life reveals a landscape filled with broken relationships or a few important relationships that are in shambles, the place to start the renovation is with God.

Forgiveness from God is the greatest gift; it's also the greatest motivator and guide for pursuing forgiveness in our human relationships. Once we know God has forgiven us, we feel compelled to forgive others. If we doubt or devalue

God's forgiveness, we won't be able to forgive others and we will probably not ask them to forgive us.

Ephesians 4:32 says, "Be kind and compassionate to one another, forgiving each other, just as in Christ God forgave you." Forgiveness isn't fair, but it is freeing.

If you have a problem with fairness, just remember that by far the ultimate unfairness is that God would forgive you. Forgiveness releases you from the "right" to get even, but it also releases you from the need to get even. If you want to see for yourself what Jesus thought about forgiveness, take a look at Matthew 18:21-35.

The most unforgettable message you can pass on to the generations following you is your own life. You will not be able to control the perceptions others have of you, but you can make it your goal, as far as it is up to you, to live at peace with others.

You can focus on your relationship with God, which will not only affect in many ways the way you treat your bride, children, and grandchildren, but may also make your life a model for people you love—a model that transforms their eternal destiny.

Action Steps

1. Modeling is rarely as direct as coaching. Think of things you can show your grandchildren. When they are at your house, do you ask them to participate in small tasks that are part of your routine? Anything from changing a lightbulb to studying the Bible to spending time in prayer can include coaching moments as well as modeling moments. Grandkids

are more likely to do as you say if they see you do as you say.

2. When I introduced the idea of legacy, I used the word *pattern* to explain how a grandfather consistently influences his grandkids over time. We create patterns for good or bad that others can see. *Modeling* is another word for patterns. What are the most significant patterns in your life, negative or positive? If you can't think of any, it's time to set out on a journey of discovery.

   Choose three people. Make sure two of them are family or close friends who have known you a long time in various circumstances. And choose at least one person who knows you well in an area where you spend a lot of time (your workplace, where you volunteer, your church). Schedule a conversation with each one, telling them that you need their help to recognize the positive and negative patterns in your life.

   Be prepared to hear the good and the bad, and decide ahead of time to listen without explaining or excusing. Resist defensiveness. Thank your friends for their honesty, even if some of the glimpses of yourself are disappointing. Discovering things about ourselves we can't see does hurt, but it can help us in the long run.

3. Write down the names of three or more people to enlist for the second action step. Then call each one.

CHAPTER TEN

DOORKEEPERS AND ELDERS

I HAVE TWO DISTINCT kinds of memories of my dad. The most powerful and consistent ones are those in which he is pulling me aside and schooling me about some aspect of life.

Not a day goes by that an event or circumstance doesn't cause me to think about a phrase he said or some counsel he gave me. But I am also struck by the vivid memories I have of my dad interacting with other men.

When I open that photo album, so to speak, the earliest pictures show me playing on the floor or hanging out as a young man at my home, vaguely aware that Dad has friends over. They are sitting in the yard, on the porch, or in the living room. Since these are more like memory videos, they come with sound.

I remember a kind of deep male hum in the background as these friends talked together, one speaking and the others agreeing or questioning with nothing more than a gravelly "Hmmm" or "Huh?" There were also frequent outbursts of laughter, with a phrase or two said in that kind of voice that combines words and chuckles, followed by a return to a deep humming you could almost *feel* if you were in the room.

I'm having a hard time describing this on paper, but if you've been around men who have known each other for a long time, you probably know what I'm talking about.

In a way, it reminds me of the difference between watching my granddaughters and my grandsons play. Granddaughters aren't generally noisy, but they are busy. And almost as soon as they learn to talk, they speak to each other while they are playing house, store, or school, but generally quietly. They are always having conversations.

The grandsons make noise. They have a hard time playing quietly. And they display a fascination with various sounds. They hold a car or airplane in their hands and immediately start making the honking, revving, and speed noises that go with that toy. Little boys almost instantly recognize the humor in body sounds (little girls think they're funny too).

Grown men and grandfathers still delight in sounds. Their conversations are less coherent and complete when compared with the extended sentences and statements of women.

Put fifteen women in a room and you will probably count sixteen or more conversations going on at the same time, because women are generally comfortable talking over, around, and next to one another at the same time. Put fifteen men in the room and one guy will ask where the remote is and when the game will start. Guys interrupt each other in conversations, but usually only one guy talks at a time.

In any case, my impression from listening to my father interact with other men all those years ago was that they simply enjoyed being together. There was an easy camaraderie, even in silence. The laughter was rich and deep. As a boy, I felt drawn into that atmosphere of shared life experience. The richness of wisdom was so obvious, I had a feeling I could absorb it just by being in the room.

It's an important moment when a young man is admitted into the circle of men. He's in, but that doesn't mean he should say anything unless he's asked a question. He needs to learn the silence and the humming first.

I'm sharing these memories because they remind me of two important roles: doorkeepers and elders. These two words describe the roles older men need to fill in their families and in society.

First, let's talk about the biblical meaning of these specific responsibilities. In Bible times, elders and gatekeepers were recognized roles that came with a lot of authority in the community.

Like many ancient great cities, Jerusalem had a massive surrounding wall that protected the population. The weakest points in a wall were always the gates, and the men stationed in those locations were responsible for the safety of many.

They had to decide who was worthy to enter and who needed to be turned away from the city. If the gate came under attack, they had to be ready to place themselves in the gap as a human gate protecting the city.

Interestingly, the city's gatekeepers and elders often spent quite a bit of time together. Traditionally, the main gate was also the place for public meetings and where community matters were discussed and settled.

There's a great example of this in Ruth 4:1-2:

> Meanwhile Boaz went up to the town gate and sat there. When the kinsman-redeemer he had mentioned came along, Boaz said, "Come over here, my friend, and sit down." So he went over and sat down. Boaz took ten of the elders of the town and said, "Sit here," and they did so.

With twelve guys together, I'm sure there was some humming and laughing going on. Boaz needed to have a man-to-man talk with a relative, and wanted wise men to witness the conversation and weigh in if necessary.

Gatekeepers represented the alert watchers in a community; the elders embodied the combined wisdom of the city. Grandfathers can play both roles. They can keep an eye on what's happening in their extended family and then bring wisdom to bear where needed.

I think my dad understood this instinctively, because he taught us to focus on the word *watch*. He found continuous instances where this principle applied to life. He even taught me to correct my over-attentiveness to myself as a young man.

Once when I was at the height of my stardom as a high school football player, Pop took me with him to buy tires for the car. The evening before, I had played a major role in our team crushing an opponent and had even scored a couple of touchdowns. I was *watching* all right—watching the accolades and praise about me roll in!

Wouldn't you know it—the man at the tire store was a football fan. He started talking about the game the previous night. He even said something like, "And that Casey kid? Great hands, and that boy can fly!"

My dad was just nodding, examining a tire. I looked over at him and raised my eyebrows, thinking, "This is it, Dad! Tell him who I am. Let's get some glory. Maybe he'll give you an extra discount on the tires!"

Dad caught my look and returned it with a slight "No" nod. Later I realized he let me enjoy the man's comments— and he was certainly proud of me himself—but he wasn't going to "trade" on my reputation, and he wasn't going to let me think more highly of myself than I ought. He was watching the big picture, not just my immediate little corner of it.

I don't know now if my daughter Patrice learned the importance of Pop's word from me or from him directly, but I will never forget seeing the word *watch* written in bold letters just above the door handle inside her college dorm room.

Every time she went out that door she was reminding herself she was a Casey, representing her family to the world. I can easily imagine Pop pointing to that little piece of paper and saying with a smile in his eyes, "See, son. That's my granddaughter. She gets it!"

In ancient times doorkeepers watched important buildings as well as the city gates. Someone served at the building's entry to admit visitors and guard against unwanted intrusions.

In Psalm 84:10, the sons of Korah wrote, "Better is one

day in your courts than a thousand elsewhere; I would rather be a doorkeeper in the house of my God than dwell in the tents of the wicked."

This Psalm dates from the time Solomon constructed the magnificent Temple in Jerusalem. Notice how the author contrasts two places ("your courts" and "tents of the wicked") by putting a role ("doorkeeper in the house of my God") between them. Obviously, "your courts" and "house of my God" are the same place. Physically they refer to the Temple, but spiritually they are talking about God's presence.

So the Psalm is saying, "I'd rather have one day in Your presence, Lord, than a thousand anywhere else!" In fact, it says, "I'd be happy being just on the inside, manning the door," rather than spending my life in the "tents," or "living the life of those who have no interest in You, Lord."

Think about the time frame being discussed here, and then remember what Peter wrote later in the New Testament: "But do not forget this one thing, dear friends: With the Lord a day is like a thousand years, and a thousand years are like a day" (2 Peter 3:8).

In "God time," spending a day in His presence is the equivalent of a thousand years, a significantly better deal than a thousand days anywhere else.

Also, a place with doors is solid and lasting, able to stand up to whatever life brings. Tents don't have doors, and they offer meager shelter in a storm. The presence of the Lord is the ultimate shelter.

As grandfathers, you and I need to quietly and calmly remind the younger generation that we trust in the God of many generations, who never slumbers or sleeps, and who always watches over us.

We can and should be calling our children and grandchildren to faith, not with angry sermons or complaining about how everything is falling apart, but by demonstrating for them a life that trusts in the Lord.

Grandpa, are you an alert watcher for your family and a bearer of wisdom?

Opening Doors

As a doorkeeper, you also open the way for your grandkids to enter into places they might not otherwise go. You can affirm their interests and help them to experience a new part of the world.

One couple takes pairs of grandchildren on mystery trips in the summer. The parents give their permission, of course, and know where their kids are going, but the kids do not.

Their first adventure involved transporting two small-town kids to the big city for a three-day trip that included the state fair, walking around downtown (a highlight for the kids), visiting a museum, and attending a Major League Baseball game. Those were just the planned highlights.

Other amazing things happened along the way. The four of them were walking downtown and stumbled upon a large bookstore. Since they're all book lovers, they spent almost an hour browsing, and each one found a book to buy. Then the kids discovered a coffee shop up the street, which they all immediately adjourned to so they could begin to read their new books.

They also strolled along an elevated walkway over a river

in the heart of the big city. The kids were mesmerized. Both agreed that when they grew up they would want to live in a big city—and maybe Grandma and Grandpa would want to live nearby, too. That simple trip opened a doorway to a new world for those kids.

Grandpa, are you a gateway to knowledge?

Doorkeepers and Neighbors

One man I know tells a story about his grandfather that chokes him up every time he shares it.

When this man was in high school, his grandfather died. When the young man went off to college, it worked out for him to live with his widowed grandmother. That gave her a man in the house, and he ate better food. He knows he had the better deal.

Often when this college student arrived at his grandmother's house after classes, the neighbor's three little boys would be playing in the yard, and he would join them for wrestling and running around. When the boys' father would get home from work, he would often sit on the back stoop and watch the boys play before supper.

One day this neighbor called the young man over and said, "I want to tell you something about your grandfather." So the young man joined him on the steps.

"When my wife and I moved in here with our boys, we were the first black family on this all-white block," the neighbor said. "I wasn't sure how that was going to work out. Your grandpa Christensen was a pretty big and intimidating-looking man."

The young man knew exactly what this father meant.

His grandfather had been a foreman in a heavy-equipment manufacturing plant: a man used to dealing with rough men.

The father went on, "About a week after we moved in, I was in the kitchen overlooking the backyard, and I saw your grandfather come out the back door of his house and walk across toward our house. I couldn't tell what was about to happen. He clomped up the stairs and knocked on my back door. When I opened it, your grandfather said, 'Well, Mr. Wallace, I have to admit I never imagined that I would be living next door to a black man and his family in my lifetime, but here you are. So, welcome to the neighborhood.' Then he reached out and shook my hand. He kind of smiled, turned, and walked back to his house."

Mr. Wallace waited a few moments for the young man to take that in, and then he said, "You can be very proud of your grandfather, boy. He taught me what it means to be a neighbor."

That grandfather was a wise gatekeeper, and his simple act of gruffly welcoming a new neighbor on a summer afternoon touched many lives.

Will your grandchildren have a few funny and moving stories about you to pass down to their children? Start by telling them your stories and letting them be with you as often as possible.

The Neighborhood Watch

Not long ago, my bride and I took a family road trip back east to Virginia with Marcellus, his bride, and their children. Part of that adventure was another visit to that big engine

611 so the grandkids could understand why Pi-Pa always talks about trains.

Another trip highlight was driving through my childhood neighborhood. These are historic spots—at least in our family. And what makes it great for me is to watch and listen to my son's interest. Sure, the grandkids' comments and questions are wonderful too:

"You lived in that house, Pi-Pa? We haven't always lived in Missouri?"

"There was a time you didn't even know Grandma?"

But my son's desire to know his roots and the kind of people his ancestors were is a joy to me.

There are families living on the street where I grew up who remember those days. People who helped raised me are still around. It takes them a moment to connect the current me with the scrawny little kid I was back then, but when they realize it's me, their faces light up and they invariably turn to Marcellus and say, "Let me tell you about your dad, boy." And they are off with a story, usually one that is somewhat embarrassing to me.

Here's the thing about doorkeepers: Long after they are gone, their doors can still bear their names. While they were alive they guarded something valuable, and their service is remembered.

Sometimes that happens through the passing of a name from one generation to the next, or to every other generation. Giving your child your father's or grandfather's name is an honor and an expressed hope that the child will have the same traits and qualities that are associated with that name. My son Marcellus bears the middle name of his great-grandfather, Reverend Charles Marcellus Coles, a bivocational gentleman who worked as a cook on trains and pastored a flock. He could do *hard* work and *heart* work.

On the flip side, knowing that one of your grandchildren bears your name does make you want to step it up as a grandfather!

From time to time it's good to visit the cemetery where family members have been buried. Having your grandchildren with you gives you a strong sense of the passing of time and the reminder that you, too, will someday (unless the Lord calls a halt to all this) be put into the ground.

As you're looking at those names chiseled into granite and marble, think about what they left behind as a legacy, which includes you. You are a flesh-and-blood extension of their lives.

I'm reminded of Paul's words to Timothy, his son in the faith, as he was considering the last days of his life on earth: "Guard the good deposit that was entrusted to you—guard it with the help of the Holy Spirit who lives in us" (2 Timothy 1:14). Paul was talking mainly about the deposit of the gospel and faith, but I'm asking you to consider "the good deposit" in another way.

Each of us carries through life a deposit in the form of our heritage. Are you guarding the good aspects of that heritage? And are you trusting in God's Spirit to help you increase the value of that heritage, to shape the legacy you'll be passing on to your children and grandchildren? That's a doorkeeper question.

Elders and Wisdom

I heard about a grandson who had recently learned to count. He phoned his grandfather to wish him a happy birthday and asked, "Grandpa, how old are you?" When his grandfather answered, "Eighty," the boy thought for a moment and responded, "Did you start at one?"

Grandpa, we have to be more than old. We need to be wise, and a wise man knows what he doesn't know.

Show your grandchildren how to learn by asking them to teach you. Ask them, "What are you learning in school these days?" If your grandchildren help you set up your newfangled electronic device, tell them, "You can never be too old or too young to learn," and then demonstrate a teachable attitude.

As an elder, you've obviously seen a whole lot more of life roll by than your grandkids have. You are living history, so be ready to talk about what you've seen, especially things that happened before they were born. And remind them you were their age once. Tell them what you remember.

I heard about one set of grandparents who spent an entire evening sharing stories of their childhood with their granddaughter.

"In the winter we used to sled on the hill and skate on the frozen pond behind the house," Grandpa said. "And in the summer we rode our pony, swung on the tire swing over the pond to go swimming, and picked wild blueberries and raspberries in the woods."

Meanwhile, the little girl sat there in wonder, occasionally saying, "Really?" After an hour of stories she exclaimed, "I wish I had gotten to know you sooner!"

Wisdom is not about how *much* you know, but how *well*

you know some things. In the old days, fathers and grand-fathers taught the next generation the tools and the tricks of their family trade. Certain kinds of work ran in families because grandkids made great apprentices.

I sometimes wonder what my two preacher grandfathers must think of the places I've preached in and the style I've developed. I believe the opportunities I have are the Lord's blessing on the lives of my ancestors.

So think about what you know well. Tell your grandkids about it. You may have to show them all the steps you take to do something they might think is magic. Let them know Grandpa feels good about doing a job well.

A grandfather who had a career in sheet-metal work for the heating and air-conditioning industry is meticulous with ducting. After he retired, he had a second career working with metals for airplanes. He was wise in the ways of sheet metal. He has a grandson who's a mechanical engineer, work-ing with (you guessed it) various metals.

Elders, Poise, and Stability

Along the highways and byways of life, things go wrong and it's easy to get frustrated. You know it. I know it. Flights leave late. Cell phone batteries die. People on the freeways curse and gesture like crazy.

When I'm in those situations, I try to ask myself, *What would my pop say?* When things didn't go my way as a child, he would tell me, "Son, don't lose your mind. Keep your poise." And he would paraphrase the King James version of Isaiah 26:3: "Thou wilt keep him in perfect peace, whose mind is stayed on thee: because he trusteth in thee."

I have to admit that when my dad said, "Keep your mind stayed on Thee, and you will be kept in perfect peace," those wise words didn't click. As a kid, I was more concerned about whatever issue or selfish thing was in my brain at the moment.

But Pop's words stuck with me. He made a deposit in my life, even though I didn't realize at the time how valuable it was.

Now that I'm in my sixties, I'm learning that a big part of my role as a father and grandfather is exactly what Pop described: to keep my poise. My son Chance and my grand-kids—and even my adult kids and their spouses—look to me for that stability.

In this world, things are always changing. People have a spirit of fear, causing them to talk down to others and lash out about small things. Plain and simple, they don't have their minds and their hearts on Christ.

As dads and granddads, we must be set apart from the standard fearful response all around us. And like my pop said, it begins by fixing our minds on the Lord, because He's the One who gives perfect peace. But Isaiah also said that the Lord's peace comes to those who trust Him.

Doorkeepers keep the passage to trusting God open in a family, and elders offer reminders and encouragement along the way to keep trusting the Lord.

We'll go through challenges and even defeats as husbands, as leaders, as fathers. Sometimes our kids are going to "lose their minds," and there's little we can do about it. They will make choices we don't agree with. And sometimes after consulting us and making good choices, things will still take turns we didn't expect.

But we have to maintain our poise. They are watching to see how we will respond. They want and they need stability from us. We show them we can cast our cares on God, and it's going to be all right because He cares for us. We *can* and *do* trust Him.

Even as an adult, when I would visit my dad and sometimes complain about the plane being late, he would set me straight. He would say, "Well, Son, the plane landed safely. So it's all good."

Right again, Pop. He was keeping his eyes on the big picture rather than the little problem and was encouraging me to do the same.

Too often we take God's blessings for granted. We're looking for something else for ourselves, and we don't notice what He has already provided—and what He has protected us from. But His blessings are there, and we need to point those out to our kids and grandkids.

I have to live like my parents, Sarah and Ralph, just as they lived out the pattern set by their parents, my grandparents. All the stories I've told about them in this book were often not meaningful events or lessons at the time, but have become sweeter and more precious to me as I've moved through fatherhood into grandfathering.

My parents were champions. They left me what I consider a mighty legacy. And they didn't do it for fanfare or to be in the newspaper or on the radio like their son is. I'm not wealthy, but my parents never made the money I make. I'm not famous, but they were never able to visit the places I've been to or be with people I've been privileged to know. Dad went to Washington to hear Martin Luther King Jr.'s "I Have a Dream" speech; I've been in the White House to meet with a president of the same race as Dr. King, a partial fulfillment of that dream.

In their lifetime, my parents weren't noticeable in the crowd, but they did "walk the talk" day in and day out. And that's the secret. They guarded their heritage of consistent, daily habits of integrity and character. They added to that heritage and passed it on, helping their children and grandchildren build those same habits and patterns.

That's what doorkeepers and elders do—they guard something precious for the next generations and do everything they can to pass it on.

We're not asked now to stand at a literal gate as in Bible times, but that doesn't mean we can cast away the roles of doorkeepers and elders. The quality of social interaction in society today and the education of the next generations are lacking because many of us have failed to act our age.

For the sake of our families and society, we desperately need more grandfathers who will accept their duty at these posts. Will you be one of them?

Action Steps

1. How much humming and laughter do you experience in your interactions with other men? Is there someone you can invite to read and discuss *Championship Grandfathering* with you?

2. You may attend a church where the elder role is clearly defined. Read 1 Timothy 3:1-7 and Titus 1:5-9. Paul told Timothy and Titus to appoint

certain men to the position of elder and then specified the qualities those men were to exhibit. Here's the point: The men appointed were already acting like elders, they weren't men who were randomly chosen to develop into leaders. Sure, we're all growing and learning (or at least we should be), but the actions of an elder need to be lived out whether or not the person has the formal title. The role of elder/gatekeeper has to be assumed long before anyone recognizes it. Grandpa, how willing are you to live as an elder/gatekeeper in your family, church, and community? Read 1 Timothy and Titus, thinking about what you can do to fit the description of these roles.

3. When you are with other men, how do serious discussions get started? Do you ask an honest question or does someone else take that role? As men, most of us tend toward "lite talk" unless someone calls us deeper. Ask your friends what they've discovered about the difference between being a father and a grandfather. Pay attention. You may just learn something. Be prepared to do some humming and laughing too.

CHAPTER ELEVEN

LIVING A BLESSING

One simple but deep thought that keeps me going is the *awesome privilege* it is to be a dad and granddad. I try to soak up every minute I get to spend with my college-age son, my three grown children, and all of my grandchildren.

Are there challenges and hard times? Of course there are, but I try to create a positive atmosphere within my family and be a force for good in their lives—in other words, a blessing.

The term *blessing* is one of those words we widely use but rarely explain. You and I may be quick to say "Bless you" when someone sneezes, but what do we really mean by that response or wish?

People often report they feel blessed as if everyone listening knows what they are actually talking about. Is feeling blessed the same thing as feeling good? There's an old hymn that urges, "Count your blessings; name them one by one." What is that song trying to get us to count? If we don't know what a blessing actually is, how can we count it?

If you Google the phrase "bless you," you will be led to some interesting history about that expression as it relates to a plague many years ago. Because one of the early symptoms of the illness was sneezing, the response "God bless you" was intended as a quick prayer of protection for that person. Other stories and legends also lie behind the term. But in all these explanations, you won't find anything about the true meaning of "bless" or "blessing."

Essentials

The word *blessing* shows up in the Bible fairly often, but its specific meaning must be dug out of the context. You might be interested to know that God originated blessing and that the term shows up twice in the first chapter of the Bible.

In Genesis 1:22, after He created all the animals, "God blessed them and said, 'Be fruitful and increase in number and fill the water in the seas, and let the birds increase on the earth.'" A few verses later, after creating human beings in His own image, "God blessed them and said to them, 'Be fruitful and increase in number; fill the earth and subdue it. Rule over the fish of the sea and the birds of the air and over every living creature that moves on the ground'" (Genesis 1:28).

By the end of Genesis, the pattern of fathers and grandfathers blessing their children is pretty well set, but *blessing* still hasn't been defined. Obviously, blessing originates with God, but what are we doing when we bless?

I am indebted to Neil Wilson for this definition:

To bless is to speak or deliver good into someone's life.

Every time you and I speak a word of genuine encouragement, helpful instruction, and gracious correction to someone, we are blessing him or her. When we give a useful gift or carry out a practical service for someone, we are delivering good to someone—we are blessing them.

When people say, "I feel blessed," they should probably say, "I sense that someone has done something very good in my life" or "I realize God has been very good to me." We bless people the most when we deliver the good to them God wants them to have.

A number of years ago now, Gary Smalley and John Trent wrote a wonderful book entitled *The Blessing* (Thomas Nelson, 1993). If blessing is missing in your life, this book will help you a great deal.

Using biblical examples, Gary and John spell out some of the components of a full blessing. They describe the spoken blessing but also give direction on how to deliver good into someone's life through actions as well as words.

One set of grandparents opened tax-free education accounts for their grandchildren. Each year as they are able, they put money into those accounts, not only encouraging their descendants to pursue education, but helping to make it possible.

One grandfather has given his grandson a set of age-appropriate tools every few birthdays as he's been growing up, eventually planning to hand over his own grown-up tools when the boy can handle them.

Another has made a point of kissing the top of his grandchildren's heads at some point when they are together. It's just a small gesture, but it delivers good into their lives.

Be a Blessing

I hope you see where this is going. You have the opportunity not only to give your grandchildren numerous blessings but also to *be* a blessing in their lives. If your grandchildren are ever taught the true definition of blessing, will they respond by saying, "I know what a blessing is because that's what my grandparents did for me"?

And Dad, if this idea of blessing is something new in your relationship with your children, realize that the desire for a parent's blessing is insatiable and remains no matter how old that person is. Even when your son becomes a grandfather, he will cherish a blessing from you.

If you doubt that at all, consider this. How much would you give to sit down with your own father or grandfather right now and hear him say something like this:

I want to tell you some things in the next few minutes that have been on my heart and mind to share with you for a long time. First, I love you, son. Nothing you've done in the past, are doing now, or could do in the future would hinder my love for you.

Second, I'm proud of you. I'm not just proud of what you have done but of who you are. I've seen these traits in your life that I deeply admire and

which make me delight to say, "That's my son."
[Name the traits.]

And third, these are some of the hopes and
dreams I have for your future . . .

Would you clear your schedule for a time like that with your
father?

As I talk about blessing your grandchildren, I'm not naïve
about the realities of raising kids. Like the rest of us, kids
aren't perfect. But sometimes parents are so close that they
can't see their kids' good traits. They're driving them crazy.
Maybe one is strong-willed and another can't seem to sit still
for a moment. Any number of behavioral challenges may
have parents at their wits' end.

As a grandfather, you can step in with the perspective of
a little distance. Just remember to be gentle and encouraging when talking to your kids about their children. Don't
make your grandkids into angels, but note the potential positive qualities God has designed into them. You're looking
for glimmers of how God might have wired that child in a
special way.

Also, consider the "other side of the coin" factor: Our
greatest strength may also be our greatest weakness. Instead
of labeling a child's behavior or tendency only as evidence
that they are acting badly, consider what positive trait is
being distorted into negative behaviors. For example, could
that child's tendency to be bossy mean she has leadership
potential?

Another way to be a blessing is to help your grandchildren
learn if they are struggling in school. Schools are getting

better at admitting that not everyone learns the same way, but individualized learning plans are almost impossible in an institutionalized setting. That's where you can step in.

Are you ready to create some experiences that will allow your grandkids to excel when they are feeling helpless? Grandchildren from the same family will have various interests. You need to be the designated cheerleader of everything from music to art to sports, fascinated by a mind-boggling variety of collections, and excited about future dreams you probably won't live to see come true (except from heaven).

One of our primary roles is giving blessings. The longer we're around, the more life becomes almost exclusively about speaking or delivering good into others' lives. That's what Championship Grandfathers do.

No one said that providing others with a living blessing is easy. Or uncomplicated. We live in a broken world that is wired to wreck good stuff. But you know what? As the kids grow up, they'll always remember the great feeling of having one or more people in their lives who delivered blessings.

If There Isn't a Blessing

In my work with fathers, especially young father-athletes, I have to talk a lot about "father wounds." I've known many amazing superstars in sports who are crippled emotionally and are unable to be good fathers themselves because of gaping injuries caused by their fathers.

No amount of fame, success, money, or possessions makes up for this wound. And most of the time, it isn't what Dad did; it's what Dad didn't do. I know that what that son is desperately missing is his father's blessing.

Part of me hates to admit it, but I'm looking grandfatherly these days. There's just a touch of gray here and there, mind you, but it's enough to let the world know I probably have grandchildren, and it's enough to make it easier for these athletes to see me as a father or grandfather figure. They want so badly to hear a father's words that they will accept me as a substitute.

I know I'm delivering a blessing in the finest sense when I speak the words they so desperately want to hear from my father's heart to their souls. I know it's not exactly the same, but it goes a long way in the right direction.

Grandpa, one of the objectives we have at the National Center for Fathering is to encourage and enlist other fathers in the task of creating a renewed culture of fathering in this country. The more grandfatherly you are, the more you can have the joy of speaking into the lives of young men—even total strangers—with words of blessing.

When you catch a dad doing something great with his kids, let him know you noticed and are proud of him. I'm not trying to be subtle: I want to recruit you into the growing band of brothers who are out to bless young fathers and pour blessings into the lives of grandchildren.

If you've never received a blessing yourself and your father is still alive, have him read this chapter. If he's no longer alive and you have a circle of friends like those I talked about in the last chapter, ask one of your friends to read the chapter and prepare a blessing for you. You may discover he needs you to do the same thing for him.

Grandfather's Blessing

What would cause a woman to say she loved someone she has barely met? The answer comes from Trish.

To set the scene: Years ago, Trish's grandfather, whose first name was Clinton, lived in western Kansas. Trish doesn't remember him at all, but she says to this day that she loves that man.

First, she loves him because she trusts the judgment of her mother and her grandmother, and they loved him a lot. But the main reason she loves the man is that Grandpa Clinton made one statement about Trish that has stayed with her for her entire life, even into adulthood.

Not long before he passed away, and when Trish was still very young, her mother took her to see her grandfather, who had suffered several heart attacks and was not doing well. As the story goes, Trish's grandmother set her on her grandfather's lap and left the room for a few minutes.

Clinton set his granddaughter on the floor, and then got on his hands and knees to crawl along with her and watch what she was doing.

When Grandma came back in the room, of course she scolded Clinton. He wasn't supposed to be out of his chair, much less crawling on the floor.

But Clinton looked up and said, "Aw, babe, isn't she the sweetest thing you ever did see?"

Trish's grandma told that story often through the years, and Trish loved hearing it. Sure, she felt loved by other people in her life. But there was something special, almost magical, about that statement from her grandfather.

Whenever she has felt down or doubted herself over the

years, she'd remember what Grandpa Clinton said about her. It always made her feel good to know there was someone out there who thought she was the sweetest thing he ever saw.

I don't know of any better way than this true story to demonstrate the power of words of blessing. As a dad and granddad, you have that power. We might often think our kids are barely listening, but when there's so much potential for good, we'd be wise to speak words of blessing and admiration to our children and grandchildren as often as we can. Spread it like seeds of love.

God might use something we say today to encourage a child for the rest of his or her life.

Enjoy the Blessing

When you are a grandparent, be ready to receive plenty of blessings for yourself! Even when those grandkids are very young, they will speak and deliver good into your life. Having a little child hug your neck with arms that can barely reach around and say, "I wuv you, Grapa," is definitely a special blessing.

Not long ago, Melanie and I welcomed all of our grandkids to our house—and none of their parents were around. It's really more work for Melanie than for me, but we both just love the opportunity.

The way she describes it, it's like "Camp Casey." She moves them around from activity to activity, from "cafeteria" time to recreation time to quiet time, and then starts all over again. Those nine grandkids are still young enough to need a significant amount of direct supervision.

On that day, I walked in after work to discover this chaos. But it's a wonderful chaos. First I visited the kitchen, and two grandkids were in there eating. They looked up at me with those big eyes, and I gave each one of them a hug and a kiss—while trying not to get messy myself. In the living room, two more were sitting together in my recliner, watching a kids' TV show. So I gave them high fives, and they took their eyes off the program long enough to give me a smile.

So I thought, *All right. I'll go change into my gym shorts and be camp coach.* But Melanie stopped me in my tracks.

"Oh, no, you can't go in the bedroom," she said. "Some of the kids are sleeping in there."

So here's the score: The man of the house comes home, but he can't sit in the kitchen because there's a booster seat fastened to his chair, his recliner is filled with two other little ones, and his bedroom is off-limits.

And if the man of the house knows something about Championship Grandfathering, he realizes this is a sweet moment. He's been shown his place in the scheme of things, and he loves it. He may gruffly mumble about the displacement, but the kids all know he's just being Grandpa, the lovable bear. He looks over the scene and, smiling, says to his bride, "We are blessed, babe."

Now I know some young parents experience that kind of chaos all day, every day. They look forward to getting some relief. That's one nice thing about being a granddad: After one evening or a couple of days, you can send the kids home and get your life back.

And when you return those grandchildren, you can encourage dads with young kids to hang in there. Remind them that children are one of God's greatest gifts. Believe it or not, someday they'll look back and miss those days. Encouraging those dads includes keeping the kids for a weekend and giving their parents a well-deserved break.

Young children certainly need plenty of time and attention—and living space—but their energy is contagious. The way they look at the world is a great reminder for our older, cynical eyes. Kids are great at repurposing furniture into various other uses: Tables, couches, chairs, and blankets become tents, castles, cars, and spaceships. Cardboard boxes we planned to flatten and recycle are fashioned by little hands into tunnels, houses, building blocks, and hiding places. A messy house becomes the new normal, and it's all part of the blessings they deliver in your life!

Granddad, it's time to not only be a blessing in these young lives, but to soak in all the good things those grandkids bring with them.

Action Steps

1. Early in this chapter, I described a conversation you might like to have with your father. Would you be willing to share similar thoughts with your children and grandchildren? You might need to write them first. That way you won't forget what you're saying in the moment, and you can hand your loved one a signed and dated copy they can keep and read in the future.

2. Make a list of your grandkids' names under the heading "Blessings in Progress." Beside each name,

describe what you are specifically doing to speak or deliver good into that child's life. Give special attention to the names with blanks behind them. True blessings are intentional, though we can't predict the size or duration of the impact.

3. Your kids and grandkids need your blessing. They may not know it or expect it, but it will change them when it comes. The words and actions that bless come with the most power when they are directed by the ultimate source of blessing, God Himself. Make it your habit when (not if) you pray for each of your grandkids by name to also say, "And Lord, make me a blessing in _____'s life."

CHAPTER TWELVE

YOU'LL GO FIRST

STATISTICALLY, you will probably leave this world before your bride does.

Back when you said, "Till death do us part," the last thing on your mind was the possibility that your death would separate the two of you, but that's the way it often is. My mom outlived my pop by eight months.

I'm not trying to upset you, but the clock is winding down, and when the time is up, your moments on the field will be over.

Clock Management

One of the marks of great teams and coaches is the way they account for the time left in a game. The term used is *clock management.* In college and professional football as well as basketball, clock management is taken to ridiculous extremes. Football has its two-minute drill and basketball sometimes stretches the last fifteen seconds of a game into an eternity of fouls, free throws, and set plays.

Claiming victory on the last play of the game or watching the ball drop through the hoop as the buzzer goes off represents some of the most thrilling moments in sports. But how do these moments compare with life?

Can you play the game of living without thinking about the clock until the last few minutes? Is it possible or even wise to assume that you will tie up all the loose ends just before the buzzer with a few choice apologies and some nice parting gifts?

Too many men think this way: *I've got to work hard so I can play when I get older and leave an inheritance to my kids, even though I hardly know them.*

I've met few grandfathers who think they have handled their time on this earth just about right. But I've heard more than one man in his dying days admit that if he had been more aware of how quickly time was passing by, he would have changed how he prioritized his hours.

Our real problem isn't that we work too hard or play too hard; our problem is that we work and play *too much.* We allow certain legitimate priorities (like a job) to *function* as the most important things in our lives, even though we may say our marriage, kids, and grandkids are just as important.

We communicate our priorities not by what we say but by what we do. If we don't actually devote any time to what we say are significant aspects of our lives, our actions will contradict our words. And know this: Our loved ones can tell the difference between actions and mere words.

Counting Days

One of the Psalms bears Moses' name. It's an amazing song about how great God is. In the middle of that Psalm is a little prayer I think about almost every time I hear someone mention clock management: "Teach us to number our days aright, that we may gain a heart of wisdom" (Psalm 90:12).

Moses wasn't talking about knowing what day your bride's birthday is, though a wise man knows that date as well as his wedding anniversary. And he wasn't suggesting we track our age carefully, so we know when we can start claiming a senior discount.

He was thinking about clock management in the game of life, not knowing exactly when the fourth quarter will be over but realizing that every sunset brings us one day closer to hearing the final whistle blow.

Numbering our days "aright" doesn't mean obsessing about death or dying. It's being realistic about how life unfolds. If you've passed the fifty-year mark, you have more years behind than ahead of you. That's a reality check.

Good clock management in a game is about deliberate moves, not frantic actions. Teams that do well in a two-minute drill are teams that have repeatedly practiced two-minute drills. Everyone knows what's expected during those precious seconds. Receivers all know that the sideline stops the clock and saves or substitutes for time-outs.

While working on this book I have also been feeling the loss of a longtime friend and mentor, Danny Lotz, the son-in-law of Billy Graham and husband of Anne Graham Lotz. He was my mentor early in ministry and had a huge hand in blessing my life. He's a man I have counted in my circle of elders and doorkeepers for a long time, and I will miss his wisdom.

He married into a high-visibility family, but he had an amazing ministry behind the scenes, supporting his dynamic bride with God's call on her life and quietly shepherding younger men like me along the way, outside the spotlight.

When I went back east for his funeral, I was struck by how deep and wide his influence was in others' lives. His life was a blessing to many.

But life doesn't have a mandatory stoppage at the two-minute time mark to alert us that the half or the game is almost over. That's why Moses' first word in Psalm 90:12, "Teach," which is directed to the God who made us, is so important.

Here's how David demonstrated in a different Psalm that God was teaching him about numbering days: "My times are in your hands" (Psalm 31:15). And what about this further thought: "All the days ordained for me were written in your book before one of them came to be" (Psalm 139:16)?

We can ask God to teach us to number our days, because He knows to the second how long our life will be. That doesn't mean God will tell me I have 362 days, four hours, and fifteen seconds left on this earth; it means He can drive home in my heart and mind the knowledge that nothing will happen to keep me from having the *exact* amount of time He has decided I should have.

Because He knows this, I don't have to worry about the

length of my life. Jesus asks us, "Who of you by worrying can add a single hour to his life?" (Matthew 6:27).

So numbering our days "aright" isn't about trying to create more of them. It's about making sure we use each day God gives us as best we can. Every day can be greeted with the same profound declaration, "This is the day the LORD has made; let us rejoice and be glad in it" (Psalm 118:24).

You can definitely memorize this verse with your grandkids. Tell your family that whatever is happening in the house, anyone has your permission to play the Psalm 118:24 card and remind everybody else what being together is all about.

Heart Exchange

Now let's return to Moses' prayer. His desire was that he would "gain a heart of wisdom" by the time God was done teaching him. Grandpa, hum a little over that one. Let it settle in.

The world likes to tell us to trust our heart, but God's Word gives us a much more realistic view. Jeremiah wrote, "The heart is deceitful above all things and beyond cure. Who can understand it?" (Jeremiah 17:9).

That sounds almost pessimistic. God was saying through Jeremiah that more than anything else, our hearts are untrustworthy, conniving, and treacherous—and can't be fixed.

It seems that we don't need a heart *change*; we need a heart *exchange*! Notice that Moses didn't ask God to teach him so his heart would gain wisdom, but so he might gain a wise heart. Jeremiah echoes this picture when he records this promise from God: "I will give them a heart to know me, that I am the LORD. They will be my people, and I will be their God, for they will return to me with all their heart" (Jeremiah 24:7). And the Lord told Ezekiel, "I will give you a new heart and put a new spirit in you; I will remove from you your heart of stone and give you a heart of flesh" (Ezekiel 36:26).

This significant point reminds me of a story about a grandfatherly Jewish rabbi who was teaching a Scripture lesson to a crowded table of young boys. They happened to be talking about Deuteronomy 6:4-9, a passage I often refer to when talking to fathers:

> Hear, O Israel: The LORD our God, the LORD is one. Love the LORD your God with all your heart and with all your soul and with all your strength. These commandments that I give you today are to be *upon your hearts*. Impress them on your children. Talk about them when you sit at home and when you walk along the road, when you lie down and when you get up. Tie them as symbols on your hands and bind them on your foreheads. Write them on the doorframes of your houses and on your gates. [emphasis mine]

One of those observant boys said, "Teacher, in verse six it tells us that God wants us to keep His commandments upon our hearts, right?"

The teacher looked at him with a twinkle in his eye and said, "You are correct, young man."

Then the boy said, "But I would think God would want

us to keep His commandments in our hearts, not just upon them. So why 'upon' and not 'in,' teacher?"

With all the boys' attention riveted on him, the teacher thought for a moment and then said, "What you have noticed is very important, son, and I don't want any of you to forget this. God knows what our hearts are like. He reminds us many times in His Word that our hearts are very hard, like stone. When we keep His commandments upon our hearts, He can crack our hearts open, and the commandments can fall in and then do their work in us."

On your way to gaining a heart of wisdom, how much heart cracking has God had to do? Because leaving a legacy of love all boils down to what *God does* in you and me, Grandpa, not what *we do* for God.

Go First

When I think about all I've encouraged you to do in this book and what I tell fathers to work at almost every day, I'm often struck by what we're up against.

We look like a high school JV defensive line facing the offensive line of a Division I college team. "Outweighed and outmatched" doesn't quite capture how ill-equipped we are to deal with the problems we must overcome.

First, there's the human condition. The world seems headed toward hell in a handbasket—mounted on a rocket. Second, we're part of a society seemingly intent on ridiculing or wiping out any mention of God, particularly the God of the Bible. And third, by the time we get serious about intentional fathering and grandfathering, we are often caught in a maze of family dysfunctions, conflicts, and crises for which there seems no obvious workable solution.

But behind and before everything else are you and me and what has to happen in us before we can expect it to happen in anyone else.

That's why the title of this chapter, "You'll Go First," has a dual meaning: It's not only about facing the reality of our physical death, but also knowing that change has to start with us. Who will go first?

Out in the world, people want to solve problems and change situations from the outside in. If we pass a law that affects everyone, then everyone will have to change. If we start a government program anyone can apply for, then everyone will benefit and the problem will be solved.

It's not that there isn't a place for the rule of law and the power of responsible government, but these things, as good and well-meaning as they might be, can't do much if hearts are hard and individual people do not change.

Real and lasting change happens just the opposite way: from the inside out. It starts with gaining a heart of wisdom. It begins when someone goes first. There might be several ideas in this book that are new to your family, or maybe just a few things. Who will introduce these changes to your family?

Who will sense that God is willing to do some amazing things through someone who is simply available? Will you put the insights and suggestions from these pages upon your heart and then ask God to break it?

Apart from what anyone else is doing in your family right now, Grandpa, are you willing to pray Moses' prayer: "Lord, teach me to number my days as I should, that I may gain a heart of wisdom"?

Start there. You go first.

Be Ready

Members of our elite military units are trained to have one item nearby. Even when they are off duty or on leave, they always have a "go bag" packed. In that duffel bag or backpack they keep all the essentials they would need during a rapid deployment.

What actually ends up in a "go bag" changes over time. In the beginning, the bag almost always has a few unnecessary items while some important things are missing. It takes experience to refine a "go bag" that works for you.

In many ways, I think of this book and *Championship Fathering* as guides to packing a "go bag" for fathering and grandfathering. In the previous book, we included age-specific activities for fathers and their children, and here I've tried to offer ideas you can adapt for grandchildren of various ages.

Because my bride, Melanie, is a teacher, she has all kinds of things stashed away for grandchildren visits. I have to admit that she's a grandmother with more than a "go bag." She has a "go house"! She sets the bar high for me to step up in my role as a grandfather.

Grandpa, are you ready to be deployed for your grandkids at a moment's notice?

Remember when you were raising your kids and the schedule on the calendar would just get crazy? Do you remember wishing you had a helping hand? Can you recall feeling outnumbered or burned out and just needing someone to step in for a little while? And don't forget the small disasters that happen when one mate is out of town, two kids are sick, and then the refrigerator dies.

Those kinds of days are likely to happen to your grown kids, too. Grandpa, you could be the solution to their problem. True, they may not call you in an emergency or a minor complication. If they don't, will it simply be their choice or will it be because they don't think you would be ready or willing to respond?

You need to show your kids you are eager to answer that call. Are you close enough and willing to cover when your kids' families, or even other families you know, need some extra help? It might be a good idea to have more than your car keys handy for such a call.

Or maybe you need to compile a list of "go-to" things around the house that are age-appropriate and ready to be used if one or more of your grandkids show up in an emergency drive-by drop-off. When you demonstrate you are willing and ready, you give your kids a greater incentive to depend on you.

Realize that your kids don't want to look inept in front of you. They dread the feeling that you would think they are bad or poor parents. That may be why they don't let you help as much as you would be willing to. If you suspect that dynamic may be at play, it would be good to tell them how much you and your bride treasured the help you received when you were young parents.

Know that your adult children need your blessing on their parenting. But what you need to avoid at all costs is any message communicating this:

We approve of what you're doing and how you're doing it because you're doing it just like us.

They need to know you recognize the challenges they are facing—challenges you never had to deal with—as well as your overall intention to always be in their corner.

You may get a little frustrated waiting "in the wings," so invite the grandkids over and schedule times for family get-togethers. Open your calendar when family members are around, and tell them you want to keep up-to-date on events you can attend and ways you can be of help.

Realize you're now the backup and may not be deployed as often as you would like. But be ready with your good attitude and your "go bag" packed.

Taking Care of Business

Financial author and radio host Dave Ramsey shares a concept I really like. He calls it having a love drawer. This is different from the "go bag." A love drawer isn't what you take with you when you're with the grandkids; it's about what to leave behind when you're no longer around.

Granddad, if you were to suddenly depart this earth, how easy would it be for your bride and kids to find everything they need in the hours and days that follow your death? Is there a drawer, a box, or a file that the family knows about? That drawer will have copies of important papers, including your will, insurance policies, and other legal documents.

It should contain more than that. It should also include an envelope addressed to each member of your family, starting with your bride and working your way down to the youngest grandchild or great-grandchild. Inside each envelope should be a note that begins something like this: "Just in case I didn't tell you often enough while I was with you, I want you to always remember _____."

In that note, you might want to designate a personal item or two as a gift to your loved one. These aren't major things that would be included in a will, but are fun and meaningful connections between you and your family member. There might be an art print or book in your study that has special meaning. Let that person know you have designated the item as his or hers, and then inscribe it with a note inside the cover or on the back of the item.

You can also make your departure easier for your loved ones by writing your own obituary and including the significant people, events, and dates that you want remembered. Grieving families often struggle with the task of remembering when and where Grandpa was born, and what years should be included in the biographical outline.

Don't forget the funeral—it's an amazing opportunity for you to say some things to your family they will never forget. Last words are important, and you might not have a chance to actually say them while you're alive. Make sure they are said anyway by writing them down.

I can tell you that one of the sad frustrations pastors deal with when meeting with grieving families are the unknown answers to such questions as the following:

"What was Dad's/Grandpa's favorite Bible verse?"

"What were the songs or hymns he most enjoyed singing or listening to?"

"Who was his favorite Bible character?"

And the real heartbreaker: "Can you tell me the story of when Dad/Grandpa put his faith in Jesus as his Savior and Lord?"

If we say these matters are important to us, why would we keep the people we love in the dark? Please don't use the "it's hard to talk about" excuse. If you can't talk about it, write it down and give it to your family. Next Thanksgiving, request a few minutes after the meal to share something important, and then read what you've written. It is our duty of love and faithfulness to pass on these core matters about ourselves.

Grandpa, where's your love drawer, box, or file? What's in it? Does everyone in the family know about it?

Let me emphasize that a man takes care of business, especially his final business. There are certain basics that you should handle in acknowledgment of your own mortality. At the top of the list should be a will. If you're a grandfather without a will, you are not only denying your mortality, but you are also setting up your family for added grief, confusion, and some anger when you die.

I'm guessing those are not the kind of memories you want to leave behind. So don't. Have your will and finances in order as well as the rest of your house. Show your love for your family, particularly your bride, by making something that will be hard as easy as possible.

A Good Death

My friend Neil and his bride, Sherrie, considered it a great honor to house Sherrie's elderly parents for a number of months. Sherrie's father was afflicted with dementia, and they knew his time was short.

It was sad for them to watch their loved one lose his bearings and repeat himself continuously, but Sherrie's dad never forgot his family. He was able to have his kids, grandkids, and great-grandkids around during that time when life was clearly coming to an end.

That year, Grandpa went to the hospital in the middle of December. The entire family brought all the gifts there so he wouldn't miss Christmas. He wasn't aware of everything that happened, but his presence was important to his family.

Before he was released from the hospital, he was placed on hospice care. He returned to Neil and Sherrie's house with his bride to die. He wasn't suffering, but it was hard on the family to realize their days with him were counting down.

Nursing care came in, and Grandpa's hospital bed in the living room became the center of family life. He was positioned at the end of the dining room table. His five great-grandkids visited, and each one found a way to do something special for their great-grandpa. One, who had recently learned to read, sat on his bed and shared a book with him.

Grandpa smiled often, and he seemed to enjoy simply being surrounded by those who loved him. Everyone knew he was dying, but they treated him as just another member of the family, including him in the conversation even though he rarely said much toward the end.

His daughter (Neil's bride) did her best to honor her father and keep his request never to be put in a nursing facility. It wasn't easy to care for someone remembered as an active and practical person who was now helpless.

Even so, Sherrie now feels it was one of the best things she ever did. They were able to bless her father with a place to stay and the best care they could give—delivering good into his life right to the end.

One Saturday, several of his great-grandkids stopped by to love him in their simple ways, and that night Bob Clark slipped away into the Lord's presence. He left behind his bride, two daughters and their husbands, eight grandchildren, and eight great-grandchildren. He also left a legacy of quiet steadiness; a love of fishing, hard work, and providing for his family; and a simple confidence in God.

Reflecting on that time in their lives, Neil and Sherrie are not only glad they were able to serve in that way, they are also glad the entire family was able to participate. The great-grandkids in particular learned that life does end, but that ending can be surrounded by all kinds of hope. That's an indelible lesson. People who trust in God still grieve, but as the Bible says, we don't grieve as those who have no hope.

One way the family affirmed their hope in eternal life was to make it a practice to never say good-bye at the end of any visit with Grandpa. The last greeting was always "See you later!" Everyone understood that the phrase meant more than it usually did. It meant that if death came, there would still be a "later" in heaven.

In Bob's case, he went first. Are you prepared to go first, in every sense of the word?

Action Steps

1. Put at least one thing in your love drawer this week.

2. Call or text each of your grandkids in the next day or two and tell them, "A friend of mine told me to contact you with this important message: I love you."

3. Consider buying copies of *Championship Fathering* and *Championship Grandfathering* to keep on hand for encouragement gifts when you spot a father or grandfather acting like a champion!

4. If you know men who are exhibiting the traits of Championship Grandfathering, make it a point in the next few days to thank and encourage them. Ask them what you can pray for on their behalf, and you'll quickly realize that everyone has areas in which they can grow.

CONCLUSION

Grandpa, I trust that reading this book has been encouraging for you. I hope you have found some new ways to practice intentional grandfathering and have decided to surround yourself with other granddads so you can keep each other company in the coming adventures.

Twenty-five years ago, my friend and mentor Ken Canfield launched the National Center for Fathering. Not only has the center reached grandfather status, I realize that many of the fathers who were part of the early days of this organization alongside Ken are themselves now granddads. That includes Ken and myself, now older and hopefully wiser. It just makes sense that we spend this time thinking and helping one another in this next phase of life. But that doesn't change the center's focus, which of course will always be on fathers.

During the 1980s and 1990s, our country began paying significant attention to the declining influence of men in our society. Part of the effect of the feminist movement, alongside its effort to gain some measure of equality and value for women, was the perhaps unintended consequence of devaluing and questioning the role of men, particularly husbands and fathers. There was some backlash, not always measured, as men felt discounted.

In the midst of this, organizations such as the church and Focus on the Family maintained a steady course, encouraging all facets of family living. And while highly visible efforts (Promise Keepers, for example) brought attention to the necessary role of men in their marriages and families, groups such as the National Center for Fathering worked behind the scenes developing a strong case for the essential role of fathers.

From where I sit now as the new "Ambassador for Fathers" in our organization, it gives me great satisfaction to know that the National Center for Fathering chose faithfulness over flash. It has maintained a presence throughout our society by steadily promoting a culture of fathering—and now grandfathering.

Twenty-five years later, we can see the fruit of patient and faithful work, one father at a time. That now adds up to more than a million fathers every year whose lives have been influenced directly by the National Center for Fathering. But that impact extends further as we encourage fathers to reach out to other fathers, and as we motivate dads to see the needs of kids in their community. Several effective fathers and grandfathers, working together, can transform a neighborhood.

I often reflect on the words of one grandfather, Joshua, when he was getting to the end of his life. He was the leader of a nation, so he had a huge audience; but he made his challenge to his people a personal one. You'll probably recognize his words:

> But if serving the LORD seems undesirable to you,
> then choose for yourselves this day whom you will
> serve, whether the gods your forefathers served
> beyond the River, or the gods of the Amorites, in
> whose land you are living. But as for me and my
> household, we will serve the LORD.
>
> JOSHUA 24:15

What can you say about your household, Grandpa? I know we all want to say that our kids and grandkids are doing just fine and are on the right track. But we can't. The best we can do is set a pattern and a way before them that they can follow and return to if they wander away. That's why Joshua had to say "as for me" before he could honestly say "and my household."

Of all the pursuits that might characterize a family, what could be better than serving the Lord? I mean this. Just think of the alternatives. There are certainly plenty of examples before us of families dedicated to pursuing fame, power, wealth, and education. So how is that going for them? And how lasting or certain are any of those achievements? They can and will be gone in an instant.

Serving the Lord is an eternal investment. This side of eternity it may not look like it has gained much interest, but hearing Jesus Christ look you in the eyes and say, "Well done, good and faithful servant" will be worth whatever happens as you are serving the Lord here. Blessings on you.

As I end this book, I'm thinking of the thoughts, feelings, and scents that I associate with my grandparents. I thought they were old; now I am just as old, and now I'm in their place. One of the most powerful gifts my grandparents gave me was a sense of security. I was secure in their love and secure in their settled character. They were who they were. And they had been that way for a long time—certainly longer than I had been around.

That tenure gave them standing in my eyes and made their no-nonsense tone meaningful. They were my parents' parents, so they knew me as a kid and knew my parents as kids, which meant in my young mind that they could speak into my life with a certain authority.

Let me encourage you to speak gently but with authority into your grandkids' lives. Be funny as well as serious. Let them see what makes you laugh, and you'll discover they'll laugh with you—or maybe at you. But you will be laughing together, which is healthy.

Now that you've made it to the end of this book, let's talk again about its title. As I was writing this, I was asked if I considered myself a "Championship Grandfather." First, that's not for any of us to claim for ourselves. Others will make that call.

This book isn't about "how to call yourself a Championship Grandfather"; it's about what Championship Grandfathers do. None of us do it all. Few of us do much of it well. But all of us who are grandfathers should consider ourselves called to practice these things as best we can. The very least we can do is to do our best, with God's help, for the next generation.

Beyond Your House

As a final word, let me encourage you to look beyond your walls and your family to the needs in our society. The figures are overwhelming. Twenty million children in the United States live in fatherless homes. Many, if not most, of those kids live in grandfatherless homes for one reason or another.

You can see the needs of these children in two obvious places: in your church and your neighborhood. Pay attention; ask around. Recruit your own grandchildren to help you speak into the lives of kids who don't have someone from your generation who cares or can be involved in their lives. This is a powerful and good way in which you and your house can serve the Lord.

ACKNOWLEDGMENTS

I am thrilled and thankful to acknowledge a few men who have loved me, coached me, and modeled for me the art of Championship Grandfathering: Ralph Waldo Casey Sr. (my paternal grandfather), Charles Marcellus Coles (my maternal grandfather), Ralph Waldo Casey Jr. (my father), and Perry Philemon Little Sr. (my bride's father). I am grateful for how they taught me Psalm 78:1-4. Verse 4 says, "We will not hide them from their children; we will tell the next generation the praiseworthy deeds of the Lord."

To Neil Wilson of the Living Stone Corporation: Words cannot adequately express how much I appreciate his thoughtful and marvelous way of putting my thoughts into print.

NOTES

FOREWORD: A CALL TO ACTION
1. Carrie A. Werner, "The Older Population: 2010," 2010 Census Briefs (U.S. Census Bureau, 2011), accessed August 24, 2016, http://www.census .gov/prod/cen2010/briefs/c2010br-09.pdf.

CHAPTER 3: ENTER THEIR WORLD
1. Kirk Bloir, "What About Grandfathers?," Ohio State University Extension Senior Series, Ohio Department of Aging, accessed December 1, 2015, http://ohioline.osu.edu/ss-fact/0195.html.
2. Ken Canfield, "Grandfathers: Leave a Lasting Legacy," blog, National Center for Fathering, accessed August 14, 2016, http://www.fathers.com /s6-your-kids/c36-grandchildren/grandfathers-leave-a-lasting-legacy.
3. Ibid.
4. Ibid.

CHAPTER 4: 611: SHOW THEM YOUR WORLD
1. Vern Bengtson with Norella M. Putney and Susan Harris, *Families and Faith: How Religion Is Passed Down across Generations* (New York: Oxford University Press, 2013), 99–112.

CHAPTER 5: CHANGING YOUR GRANDKIDS' HERITAGE
1. Bengtson with Putney and Harris, *Families and Faith*, 99–112.
2. Carey Casey, *Championship Fathering* (Wheaton, IL: Tyndale House Publishers/Focus on the Family, 2009), 14.

CHAPTER 7: A LEGACY OF LOVING
1. Gary Chapman, *The Five Love Languages* (Chicago: Northfield Publishing, 1992).

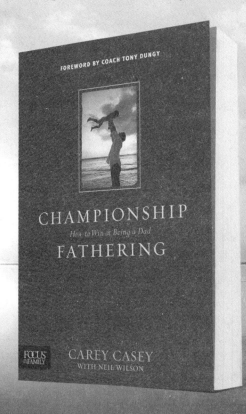

Meet the rest of the family

Expert advice on parenting and marriage . . .
spiritual growth . . . powerful personal stories . . .

Focus on the Family's collection of inspiring, practical resources can help your family grow closer to God—and each other—than ever before. Whichever format you need—video, audio, book, or e-book—we have something for you. Discover how to help your family thrive with books, DVDs, and more at **FocusOnTheFamily.com/resources**.

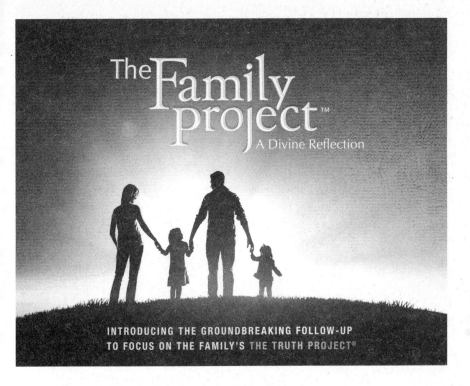

The**Family**
project™
A Divine Reflection

**INTRODUCING THE GROUNDBREAKING FOLLOW-UP
TO FOCUS ON THE FAMILY'S THE TRUTH PROJECT®**

THE PROFOUND IMPACT OF BIBLICAL FAMILIES

From the creators of the life-changing series *Focus on the Family's The Truth Project* comes a stunning, new journey of discovery that explores family as a revelation of God—and the extraordinary impact families have on the world around them. Introducing *The Family Project*, a transformative feature-length documentary and DVD small-group experience that reveals—through an in-depth exploration of God's design and purpose— biblical truths about the role of families in society.

**VISIT
FamilyProject.com
TO LEARN MORE**

A PROGRAM OF FOCUS ON THE FAMILY®